God is in the habit of using broken fam
Family, Jessie vulnerably and authentically shares the power of
that truth through her own story and then effectively empowers
young girls to discover it for themselves. Wow. This book is for
all teenage girls who want to discover purpose and find healing
within their families; for parents who long for deeper, richer,
God-honoring relationships with their daughters; and for small
group leaders who want to bring reconciliation into the lives and
homes of their students. Grab this book, read it in community,
and expect to receive gospel truth, fresh perspectives, and life-
altering advice.

MEGAN FATE MARSHMAN
Director of women's ministries at Hume Lake Christian Camps

An easy read with lots of fun, useful, and engaging exercises for
teen girls. This book belongs in the hands of every Christian girl
trying to do the teen years right. It is biblically solid, relationally
focused, authentic, and very practical.

DANNY HUERTA
Vice president of parenting and youth at Focus on the Family

In *Family*, Jessie is honest, relatable, and completely down to
earth. She doesn't shy away from sharing the good, the bad, and
the ugly about her own family and growing-up years. She gives
you an honest inside peek that not many people are willing to
give. This book is filled with solid biblical truth and practical
advice on how to love and live with your family well. Jessie
is the big sister that every teen girl wishes she had. We highly
recommend this book!

KRISTEN CLARK AND BETHANY BAIRD
Founders of GirlDefined Ministries and authors of *Girl Defined: God's
Radical Design for Beauty, Femininity, and Identity*

Jessie has done it again! She's written an easy-to-read and down-to-earth, practical guide for getting along with your family. She doesn't pull any punches as she shares the joys and pains from her own family. It's a must-read experience of changing attitudes, forgiveness, and looking ahead to your future family . . . and you will laugh when you meet Mr. Big Toe.

BOB PHILLIPS
Licensed therapist, director emeritus at Hume Lake Christian Camps, and bestselling author

At our residential program for struggling teens, we are constantly looking for great resources. Many teens come to us when their family relationships are at their worst. After reading Jessie's book, I had to wonder, *How many of our girls would have even needed to come to us if they had read Jessie's book when things at home began to get tough?* Jessie uses stories and questions to help readers deal with the pain of their own family brokenness. And then she leads them through the process of finding forgiveness, redemption, perspective, and hope. We will be getting a copy for each of our girls at Shelterwood!

JIM SUBERS
President and CEO of Shelterwood Academy

Jessie Minassian has a high calling in connecting with teen girls about the issues closest to their hearts. In this vulnerable, practical, and thoughtful book, she speaks to that perennial struggle of every teen: how to relate to family through the good and bad. She helps teens understand their families better—while also giving girls tools to better connect and find understanding in an often fraught relationship. This book is an excellent and much-needed resource for every teen girl.

DAVID EATON
CEO and cofounder of Axis

Family

How to LOVE yours
(and help them
like you back!)

JESSIE MINASSIAN

A NavPress resource published in alliance
with Tyndale House Publishers, Inc.

NAVPRESS ●

NavPress is the publishing ministry of The Navigators, an international Christian organization and leader in personal spiritual development. NavPress is committed to helping people grow spiritually and enjoy lives of meaning and hope through personal and group resources that are biblically rooted, culturally relevant, and highly practical.

For more information, visit www.NavPress.com.

Family: How to Love Yours (and Help Them Like You Back)

Copyright © 2017 by Jessie Minassian. All rights reserved.

A NavPress resource published in alliance with Tyndale House Publishers, Inc.

NAVPRESS and the NAVPRESS logo are registered trademarks of NavPress, The Navigators, Colorado Springs, CO. *TYNDALE* is a registered trademark of Tyndale House Publishers, Inc. Absence of ® in connection with marks of NavPress or other parties does not indicate an absence of registration of those marks.

The Team:
Don Pape, Publisher
Caitlyn Carlson, Acquisitions Editor
Nicole Grimes, Designer

Cover illustration by Nicole Grimes. Copyright © Tyndale House Publishers, Inc. All rights reserved.
Cover typeface Asphalts © by The Branded Quotes. All rights reserved.
Rubik's Cube® and image used by permission of Rubik's Brand Ltd. www.rubiks.com.
Author photograph by Paul Minassian, copyright © 2017. All rights reserved.

Published in association with the literary agency of Wolgemuth & Associates, Inc.

Unless otherwise indicated, all Scripture quotations are taken from the *Holy Bible*, New Living Translation, copyright © 1996, 2004, 2015 by Tyndale House Foundation. Used by permission of Tyndale House Publishers, Inc., Carol Stream, Illinois 60188. All rights reserved. Scripture quotations marked CEV are taken from the Contemporary English Version, copyright © 1991, 1992, 1995 by American Bible Society. Used by permission. Scripture quotations marked ESV are taken from *The Holy Bible*, English Standard Version® (ESV®), copyright © 2001 by Crossway, a publishing ministry of Good News Publishers. Used by permission. All rights reserved. Scripture quotations marked MSG are taken from *THE MESSAGE*, copyright © 1993, 1994, 1995, 1996, 2000, 2001, 2002 by Eugene H. Peterson. Used by permission of NavPress. All rights reserved. Represented by Tyndale House Publishers, Inc.

Some of the anecdotal illustrations in this book are true to life and are included with the permission of the persons involved. All other illustrations are composites of real situations, and any resemblance to people living or dead is coincidental.

For information about special discounts for bulk purchases, please contact Tyndale House Publishers at csresponse@tyndale.com, or call 1-800-323-9400.

Cataloging-in-Publication Data is available.

ISBN 978-1-61291-630-9

Printed in the United States of America

23	22	21	20	19	18	17
7	6	5	4	3	2	1

To Arthur Ross Jewett (aka Daddy).

Thank you for choosing to love me as your own.

And to Erin, Ian, Henry, and Alicia.

*I love you. (And I'm glad you've liked
me back . . . most of the time.)*

Contents

Introduction

I'VE READ A lot of books—*lots* of them—and all my favorites have something in common. Each one made me feel as if I were talking with a friend, or at least someone who cared about my life. I guess when it comes down to it, I don't like having someone I've never met tell me how to live. Wild guess here—maybe you don't either? It's easier to listen to advice when we hear it from someone we know and who we know cares about us, right? (And let's be honest, sometimes it's really encouraging to hear that an author is *human*, just like the rest of us!) So before we dig into this book together, it's only fair that we get to know each other a bit.

I'm Jessie. My given name is actually Jessica, and my last name is so hard to pronounce that I avoid using it when possible. (Just for kicks, it's pronounced min-à-see-in.) My single momma brought me into this world on a beautiful Californian March day just a *few* years ago (wink). She got married when I was five, and I grew up in a blended family of five kids. (You'll get to hear more about them later.) I played lots of sports in school and tried to figure out how to love God with my whole heart when it seemed to be *way* more interested in boys. (Maybe you can relate?) I liked school when I had friends, thought it was miserable when I didn't. I got good grades, ate too many Twix for lunch, and never got used to spending ten to twelve hours a week on a school bus. (We kind of lived in the boondocks.)

After high school graduation, I went to a Christian college in Southern California. I played volleyball there and then got into rock climbing. I studied abroad two semesters, one in Israel and the other in Costa Rica. I still liked school when I had friends and learned not to be miserable when I didn't. I got fewer good grades, stopped eating Twix for lunch, and traded the school bus for my first car (a ridiculously small gold Toyota MR2). There were ups, there were downs, and then there was *him*.

I married my match made in heaven the weekend after college graduation. For now, let me just say that Paul (or "Paco," as most people know him) swept me off my feet and I have never looked back. Best friends make the best soul mates, and he was—and is—both. (*Awww!*) I didn't think I had room for any more love in my heart until God gave us two daughters, Ryan and Logan. They're sweet li'l blessings wrapped in two feisty packages!

Besides loving on my family, my greatest joy these days is to help girls find their identity, pleasure, and purpose in God. I'm the resident big sis for a website called LifeLoveandGod.com, where I answer girls' questions about

. . . well, life, love, and God. (I know, pretty creative, right?) Now that I have two daughters of my own, I'm all the more passionate about seeing girls understand their unique beauty, know how amazing God is, and hold their heads high in dignity.

That's where the LIFE, LOVE & GOD series comes in. These books are meant to be the closest thing to just hanging out at my house, going for a hike together, or meeting for a small group in my living room. Each book covers different stuff you're facing, whether it's relationships with guys, shameful addictions, body image, or getting along with your family.

You'll want to have a notebook or journal handy for the discussion questions at the end of each chapter. Trust me, you'll get so much more out of this book if you take time to think through those questions. Even better, grab a couple of friends (or your mom or a youth-group leader) and go through the book together! My heart is to see you grow in your relationship with God and shine with confidence, and that happens most often when you're in community with others.

You can find out more about my random favorite things on the "Meet Jessie" page at LifeLoveandGod.com. I'd love to hear a little about you, too, if you'd like to send me an e-mail at the website!

Now, if you're ready, let's dive into the messy, beautiful, infuriating, and comforting world of family life. I can't wait to help you love them more (and help them like you back)!

Love,

Jessie

CHAPTER ONE

The Family Secret

MY HANDS WORKED with angry determination, stuffing random items into my faded JanSport backpack. Through tears, I shoved in a pair of jeans, a sweatshirt, a surfboard necklace given to me by an old crush, two granola bars, and a few crumpled bills I'd pulled out of a wooden piggy bank. At fourteen, it felt like my family was spinning out of control, and I wanted out. Now the biggest question was whether that out would be through my second-story bedroom window or the front door. The decision kept me occupied longer than I wanted it to, and while I thought about it, my mind wandered.

I had planned my escape just that afternoon, while listening to a Depeche Mode album that had recently become my anthem. It was dark and depressing music, matching (causing?) the storm clouds that now filled my heart and darkened the sky outside my window. Dad had yelled at me again. I felt like whatever I did wasn't good enough. He seemed to get mad at me for no reason, and even though I knew my attitude had room for improvement, it all felt so unbearable. Unfair. Unreasonable. Unloving. Un-*everything*. Maybe once I was gone, he would realize that I wasn't such a bad kid.

Gone.

The word sounded both exciting and final. Would I do it? I knew I would miss my mom. Maybe my brothers and sister, too. But the thought of being free to make my own decisions—go where I wanted with whomever I wanted—filled me with a wild excitement. It ignited something in my teenage heart that felt rebellious and right all at once. Plus, I was so angry with my dad that I couldn't really think straight.

I looked at the Rollerblades leaning against one corner of my bed—my "getaway vehicle." Brilliant, right? My brother Henry had given them to me when he got a new pair, and for the past few months I had been practicing in a small, relatively flat parking lot a few miles from my house. Getting my blading legs had been slow—*really* slow. I mean, I could stay on two feet and turn wobbly circles if I wasn't going too fast, but . . . *stopping.* Oh man! In all my angst and determination, I had completely forgotten that because my brother had been into trick Rollerblading, my new wheels were missing one important feature: *brakes.*

I looked out my window again, tracing the road with my eyes. Downhill to the right, even steeper downhill to the left. And we're talking mountain roads, so when I say downhill, I mean some long, steep grades on cracked pavement. Fear suddenly replaced the tug of freedom as I pictured myself speeding out of control down Voltaire Drive on my brakeless Rollerblades, crashing in a tangled mess of bruised ego and broken bones at the bottom.

And that, my friend, was the end of my runaway plan.

Of course, it wasn't the end of the heartache I'd feel in my family. It wasn't the only time I wished I could do something to change my circumstances or just change families altogether. There were other moments when I'd wonder if things would have been different if my mom had married my biological father or if my three stepbrothers lived with us full-time or if my half sister weren't seven years younger than I am. But my decision to stay was the beginning of a long road to learning to love my family better. I figured that if I wasn't going to leave, I might as well learn to stay well.

In case you haven't caught this yet, my family wasn't perfect. And (I know this might come as a shock) I wasn't perfect either. There were nights I cried myself to sleep, wishing my parents would get a divorce because I was so sick of the fighting. There were days when I rolled my eyes, slammed doors, and probably made my parents, brothers, and sister wish they could divorce *me*. My family had some stellar strengths too—such as humor, work ethic, and devotion

When Family Is Unsafe

Right out of the gate, we need to talk about a big ol' elephant in the room. I know the statistics: Too many girls have been abused by people who should be protecting them. If you have suffered harm—emotional or physical—at the hand of a family member, I want you to know that I see you. I care about you. And because God is giving me this moment in time with you, there are a few things I want you to know before we go any further in this book.

First, the obvious: Abuse is never okay. I'm sure you have heard that before, but if you or someone else in your family is the victim of physical, sexual, or verbal abuse, I'm begging you to take action. Get safe and get help.

Second, I'm writing to a wide spectrum of girls, so as someone who's been abused, you might react to some parts of this book differently than other readers do. For example, when we talk about honoring our parents or building their trust, you might feel confused or uncomfortable. When in doubt, I want you to filter what you read through this truth: You are not responsible for the abuse, and under no circumstances should you allow it to continue. Beyond that, most of what we'll discuss in the chapters to come is universal to family, and I think you'll find some useful nuggets no matter how deeply you've been wounded in the past.

Finally, will you do something for me? If you haven't already, will you please reach out for guidance from someone you trust or who is trained to help girls work through the tangles of trauma? There is no shame in letting someone walk this journey toward healing with you. If you're not sure where to turn, you'll find resources listed at www.LifeLoveandGod.com/family. Don't hide from help. You don't have to walk through this alone.

to one another—but I'm not going to gloss over the ugly family moments that marked my growing-up years, because there's about a 100 percent chance that your family isn't perfect either. And I'm guessing that you want to know how to fix what you can and how to make it through what you can't.

As kids, we don't get to choose our families. We have no control over our family members' issues and, if we're honest, we rarely understand our own. Family can be awesome, and it can be just plain messy. There might be times when we feel secure, safe, and thankful, and other times when we feel afraid, unappreciated, and unloved.

Whether you are nothin' but thankful for your family or have a genuinely warped family life, I have some really good news and a handful of tips that will show you what it means to love your family well, how to help them like you back, and a secret plan God has for you through—not in spite of—your family.

We're going to get down to business soon, but before we do, I want you to take a few minutes to sum up your family life by taking a little quiz. Let me give you two reasons why you shouldn't skip this part: (1) It's going to help you pinpoint where you stand in your heart with your family, and (2) We're going to refer back to your answers in chapters to come, and you can't refer back if you skip this. Savvy? That said, if you're afraid someone (read: little brother) is going to find your answers or if you're going to lend this book to a friend, you can write your answers down in that journal I mentioned in the introduction and hide it in your underwear drawer.

Who's My Family?

We're going to be talking a lot about your family in the coming chapters because, well, this is a book about family and all. But "family" can mean a lot of things these days, so it might be helpful to clarify what I mean by the word. Whether you'd describe your family as blended, state enforced, stable, or pretty messed up, when I talk about your family, I want you to think of the people God has put in your life to take care of you and for you to take care of. They might be blood relatives; they might not. For example, if you don't live with your biological parents, when I talk about "Mom" and "Dad" in this book, I want you to swap those for the names of the authority figures in your life, whether they are adoptive parents, stepparents, grandparents, or even an aunt and an uncle. Same thing with your siblings. They don't have to share your DNA to count as brothers or sisters.

Mi Familia

1. This first one's easy. Draw a mini family tree of your immediate family members: parents, brothers, and sisters. *(For who counts as your family, see the "Who's My Family?" box.)*

    Now rate each of those relationships on a scale of 1 to 10 (10 being "We have a great relationship" and 1 being "I'd rather be related to President Coriolanus Snow.") Write a number next to each person's name.

2. What frustrates you most about your

    • Dad?

    • Mom?

    • Brothers and sisters?

3. What do you like most about your

   • Dad?

   • Mom?

   • Brothers and sisters?

4. From your perspective, do your parents trust you?

5. Do your parents act more like parents or friends? Do you like it that way, or do you wish they acted differently?

6. What's your favorite memory with your mom? Your dad?

7. What do you argue with your parents about?
Check all that apply, and then circle the top two.

☐ Attitude/respect   ☐ Friends

☐ Social media   ☐ Faith or what's right/wrong

☐ Boys   ☐ Food and health issues

☐ Money   ☐ Brothers/sisters

☐ Chores   ☐ Entertainment

☐ Freedom   ☐ Other:

8. On a scale of 1 to 10, rate the level of respect you show
your dad and mom, with 1 being "I can be pretty snotty"
and 10 being "I always show respect." (Put an initial above
each rating if they are different for each parent.)

1   2   3   4   5   6   7   8   9   10

9. If you could ask your parents one question about anything, what would you ask?

10. What's the most important thing you wish your parents
knew about you?

11. What do you argue about most often with your brothers and sisters?

12. On a scale of 1 to 10, rate how well you treat your siblings, with 1 being "I treat my dog better" and 10 being "I'm an All-Star Sis." (Again, you can have separate ratings; just put an initial above the number you choose for each person.)

    1   2   3   4   5   6   7   8   9   10

13. If you could ask each of your siblings one question, what would you ask?

14. If you could change one thing about your family, what would you change?

15. What's the best advice a family member has ever given you?

16. If I asked your family to tell me one thing they wished they could change about you, what do you think they would say?

17. What would you say are the ingredients to a happy, healthy family?

18. Is yours a "happy, healthy family"? If not, what do you think it would take to change your family dynamics to make it a loving, safe place?

19. What do you think other people would say is your family's greatest strength?

20. Did you discover anything new about yourself or your family by thinking through these questions? If so, what?

Thanks for taking the time to answer all my questions. I know from experience that when we're in the middle of family life, whether our family relationships are fairly healthy or need a whole bunch of work, we can have a hard time seeing the real issues and how to solve them. Sometimes it's good to take a step back from our world and evaluate why things work the way they do.

The Big Why

Why has always been one of my favorite questions (which I'm sure my parents *adored* about me). I believe that if we're willing to keep digging for answers, asking why can help us understand ourselves and the world around us better. In fact, I discovered that secret I mentioned earlier—the secret plan God has for you through your family (which I promise to share with you before this chapter is through!)—by asking some key whys. Topping the list: *Why do I exist?*

Revelation 4:11 says,

> You are worthy, O Lord our God,
>   to receive glory and honor and power.
> For you created all things,
>   and they exist because you created what you pleased.

That means everything in this life is from God, for God, and about God. For some of us, that's a hard pill to swallow. We're used to people—from teachers to parents, from friends to a gazillion advertisers—making it about us. They tell us that we should go for our dreams, make names for ourselves, do what feels good, treat ourselves like princesses, and do whatever makes us happy. So if you are (as I was) used to feeling as if the world kind of revolves around you—at least in your own mind—you're going to need a big heart adjustment for the secret to stick. This is not for the faint of heart. It's tricky to change the point from which we see the world—to move from seeing everything as it affects *me* to how I affect *others*. And the most important "other" is God.

It's all about God, from the galaxies overhead to the microscopic critters beneath our feet. He made this all for Himself—for His enjoyment, yes, but also for His glory, His greatness, and His fame.

We exist to bring God glory.

Okay, then *how*? (Coincidentally, my second-favorite question.) How do we bring God glory? Well, one way that God gets bunches of glory is when we live our lives for Him and take daily, careful steps to become more like Jesus.

In case you're wondering where in the world I'm going with this, let me assure you that this has everything to do with your family scene. See, God is in control, doesn't make mistakes, and sometimes does things that make no sense to us. And the family He has put you in? Yep, He did it on purpose. He had a reason for choosing your parents at the beginning of your life, and He has a plan for all the ups and downs since. That plan just might not be what you've thought it was up till now.

God's ultimate goal for putting you in your family isn't your happiness, although happiness might come from it. It's not to make you feel safe, though at times you might feel secure. It's not even to give you an example to follow, though you might pick up some good family habits before you leave home. His reason for choosing your family for you is way bigger than those things. He chose your family because of the secret, which I will share after one more pit stop—promise!

What about Abuse?

If you've been abused, that last paragraph might have you asking more questions. Namely, if God chose your family on purpose, does that mean He wanted you to be abused or abandoned? I mean, if God is all-powerful, couldn't He have prevented it? And because He didn't, does that mean He isn't loving? These questions, dubbed "the problem of pain" by famous theologian C. S. Lewis, might be the number one reason people reject God. And I get it. How could a good God allow such wicked things to happen in this world?

I wish we could talk about this while sitting curled up on my couch with cozy blankets so you could see the tears in my eyes as we dive into these difficult questions. When I say that God wants to use the *pain* caused by your family members, I am not saying that He wanted you to be abused or abandoned. And yes, I do believe that God is all-powerful and *could* prevent evil if He wanted to. I also believe that God is love. So how can both be true?

When God created humans, He wanted us to choose Him on our own, without being forced to love Him. Love isn't love unless it's a choice. And the only way we could choose Him is if we had something called free will (i.e., the ability to choose right and wrong). So God gave it to us: He allowed humans to choose to love Him or choose to reject Him.

God loves us so much that He respects that freedom of choice to the point of letting us make a mess of the perfect world He created. Sis, it isn't God's fault that evil runs rampant; it's ours, as a human race. When we reject God and do what seems good in our eyes, rejecting His ways and will, then we also say "no thanks" to the blessings He wants to give us. It breaks God's heart to watch us self-destruct.

Even though this seems completely backward at first glance, only a *loving* God would allow evil to exist, because it's the by-product of the free will He gave us. Only a humble God would allow Himself and His plan to be rejected by His creation.

My favorite thing about God, though, is that instead of saying, "Well, y'all made a hot mess of things, so good luck—I'm out like trout," He swept up the splintered pieces of this world and built a cross with them. He made a way to dwell with His people (through His Spirit in the hearts of those who choose Him) so He could walk with us through the pain, catch our tears in His nail-scarred hands, and promise to redeem every hard thing that has happened to us, including the evil committed against us, for His glory and our good.

So the people in your family who have hurt you are, in

their free will, saying no to God's plan for them. And that has consequences, sometimes for the people they are supposed to love the most. My heart breaks if you've experienced that. It is not what God wanted for you. But because He is good and loving, He can take what is painful and make it something beautiful. And *that* takes us right back to the secret.

The Secret

This family stuff is no joke. It can be hard and messy, painful and confusing. But it all has a hidden purpose built on the truths we've discovered through the questions we've asked: *God wants to use your family—whether it's close to perfect or completely messed up—to make you more like Jesus.*

That's His secret plan! Romans 8:29 says, "For God knew his people in advance, and he chose them *to become like his Son*" (emphasis added). That little *for* at the beginning of the verse is really important. In hermeneutics (the science of interpreting the Bible), it's called a "causal conjunction." That's fancy speak for telling us that this verse explains why the verse just before it is true. And the verse just before it is one you've probably heard before. In fact, it's one of the most read and highlighted verses in the Bible!

> And we know that God causes everything to work together for the good of those who love God and are called according to his purpose for them.
>
> ROMANS 8:28

Don't you love that verse? It's been one of my favorites for like forever. But I just recently made the connection between this verse and verse 29. I'm bursting to share it. The whole reason we know that God makes everything work together for our good is because "the good" isn't our happiness, good grades, making it on *The Voice*, winning the state championship, or even getting married. The good—the biggest good in the world—is becoming more like Jesus! And if that's true, then God has most definitely given us our families for our good. Come on, they're a perfect boot camp for becoming like Jesus, aren't they? Can you think of any better place to learn and live out Jesus' patience, obedience, selflessness, compassion, grace, forgiveness, and genuine, never-giving-up love?

Yeah, I'd say families are a great way for us to test out all that we're learning from God. All the ugly selfishness, snippy attitudes, anger, and plain ol' sin I struggle with almost exclusively show up in my own home. There's nothing like being surrounded with the same group of people, in a confined space, for lengths of time, through the stresses of life, to show us what we're really made of and where we need to grow! Amen? And for that reason, our families are a *huge* blessing.

The Foundation

My sister, Alicia, is an amazing makeup artist. Whenever she comes to visit, I get excited because, well, I love spending time with her but *also* because there's a chance I'll feel like a celebrity for a day. We've settled into this sort of mutually beneficial routine. First thing in the morning (while her nieces jump rambunctiously into bed with her), I put on a pot of coffee. To butter her up. You see, she loves coffee; the smell alone makes her happy. Then sometime after her caffeine fix and a yummy breakfast, I'll ask in my sweetest big-sister voice, "Leash, will you *pretty please* do my makeup today?" To which she never says no. I love her for this.

If you've read my book *Backwards Beauty: How to Feel Ugly in 10 Simple Steps*, then you know that I'm learning to do beauty on the cheap. Left to myself, I buy my makeup at Target, not MAC. My sister, on the other hand, has the good stuff, and it shows. Also, she has the hand of a makeup magician. Many would kill for her gift. For some reason, no matter how many times she explains the techniques, I never can get my makeup to look *quite* the same when she leaves. (Possibly a combination of shaky skills and those second-rate products I'm fond of?) I've picked up a few things during our morning makeup routine though. Topping the list: Don't cheap out on the foundation.

Foundation is to the rest of your makeup as a good sauce is to a perfect pizza. It's the base, and without a good one, your makeup is going to fall flat and rub off by noon. If you want your artistry to glow till the night hours, use a quality foundation.

The secret we just discovered is like that. It's the quality foundation for this entire book that is going to help the changes we make glow and go the distance. Not to overstate it, but this little tidbit alone might revolutionize your family life. Seriously, it just might. Because in light of the secret, the question changes from "Why can't my family make me happy?" (or understand me, or cut me some slack, or support me) to "How can I become more like Jesus through my family?" And that, my friend, is some quality foundation. As we tackle big issues in the pages ahead—stuff like forgiveness, freedom, and fighting fair—let's remember that the point of all of it is to bring God glory by learning to live and be more like Jesus. For that reason—and maybe that reason alone—I'm glad my brakeless Rollerblades kept me from making an escape after all. I wouldn't be who I am today if I had run away from the pain.

> *Dear God, I admit that sometimes I really don't understand why You've chosen to put me in the family you have, but I want to trust You. I believe that You have my good in mind, and I want to learn how to love my family better. Make me more like Jesus through the good, bad, and ugly of my family life. More than anything, I want to bring You glory! Amen.*

Application Questions

1. *Have you ever been tempted to run away? How do you think your life would be easier? Or, if you have ever succeeded at running away, did your life get easier? In either case, what got you to that point of despair?*

2. *Why do you think so many families are struggling these days?*

3. *What do you think girls in your generation would say is the point of family?*

4. *Did you discover anything about yourself or your family by taking the "Mi Familia" quiz?*

5. *According to Romans 8:28-29, what is God's ultimate "good" for your life, including your family life? (Hint: It's "The Secret"!)*

6. *Have you ever considered that the point of family might not be your happiness but rather to help you practice Christlikeness? How does that truth change the way you see your family situation?*

7. *Can you see any ways that God might be using the stuff you've faced (or are still facing) to build character in your life? If you don't yet, that's okay. I'll ask again at the end of the book!*

8. *What do you hope will change in your heart or in your family by the time you finish this book?*

CHAPTER TWO

Dreams, Meet Diaper Rash

ARTHUR AND MARYANN.

Growing up, I knew them as Dad and Mom. Funny how when we're kids we sometimes forget that the people who live with us have real names and are actual *people*—like all by themselves, not just because they're related to us.

As a teenager, I was one of the worst offenders. I viewed the world as an entire planet orbiting around me, so I never really gave much thought to the fact that my parents had had lives before I existed—and still had them, for that matter. I lived as if God created Art and MaryAnn for the sole job of raising me, feeding me, driving me around, making me happy, and providing me with spending cash. It sounds so selfish now that I see those words on paper, sticking out in all their self-centeredness. But that's pretty much how it went down.

When I moved out and started a life of my own, though, the strangest thing happened: I discovered that my parents are actually fascinating people, complete with future hopes, disappointed dreams, funny memories, inspiring strengths, and relatable weaknesses. I *like* them. Not just because they love me despite my quirkiness and still remember my birthday, but because they are interesting and witty and have a lot to teach me about life.

I know it isn't easy to see your parents objectively while you're still under their roof. Obviously, I wasn't great at it. But as one who has made it to the other side of the early adult years, for this one chapter, I want to open your mind to the possibility that there's more to your parents than meets the eye. I want you to imagine that instead of living *with* them, you're watching a movie *about* them. What kind of characters are they? What have they sacrificed? What do they hope and dream?

If you're willing to dig a little and use a big dose of imagination, by the end of this chapter I think you'll have a whole new understanding of the people who chose to take on the incredible task of raising you.

Parents Have Dreams Too

I told you I wasn't good at seeing my parents from an outside point of view. Case in point: I knew very few details about my mom's life, even though I lived with the woman, and the details I did know were mostly those that affected me in some way. But as an adult, I started to ask questions. I found out more about my mom: her dreams, courage, strength, and faith. And I was blown away by the woman I discovered. Check this lady out . . .

MaryAnn Radovan left the small midwestern town where she grew up to make a new life. Though she was a nominal Catholic, she had made some poor decisions and was ready for a fresh start. The twenty-seven-year-old wanted to show her parents and eight brothers and sisters that she had what it took to succeed. She was determined to make them proud.

She and a friend drove cross-country with their few possessions, landing near San Francisco with no job and no place to live. Talk about an adventurous spirit! And they made it work—got jobs and settled in. She was finally living the dream. But the wild life MaryAnn had been living followed her to the Golden State. Drinking. Sex. And then the unthinkable happened: *She got pregnant.*

This small-town girl who left home to live her dreams and make her family proud now faced one of the most difficult decisions a girl can ever have to make: *Should she keep the baby?*

The father didn't think so. He had his own issues he was working through. Her doctor didn't think so either. He told her that an abortion would have "the least psychological effects." Even her parents asked her to give the baby up for adoption. But MaryAnn was convinced she didn't have the right to take away a life to cover up her mistake, and she didn't think she could live with the thought that somewhere on earth her baby might wonder why her mom didn't want her. So in a great act of courage and sacrifice, despite complete fear over how she would be able to support another life, she chose to keep her baby.

Ironically and beautifully, she named the baby *Jessica*, meaning "gift from God."

A few months later, she sat on a pew in a nearly empty Catholic church with that little baby on her lap. She prayed, "God, You know how I've messed up my life. I don't know how to make good decisions for Jessica. She's Yours, God. Please show me how to offer her more hope than I have for myself. You may not want me, but please give her hope!"

Two years later, God showed MaryAnn that He *did* want her, despite her mistakes, despite her fears. She sat in her parents' home (where she had to live for a time) and asked Christ to take over her life. And He answered her prayers for her baby girl, too. That little girl—now a grown woman—has never *not* known that God loved her and wanted her. And she has always had *hope*.

It's a tearjerker, isn't it?

Instead of viewing the story of my birth in terms of how it affected me—poor me, going through life without knowing my biological father—I now see it as one of the most beautiful stories of tragedy turned to love I've ever heard. A story about courage, accepting responsibility, and God's grace poured over and through a lifestyle of shame to bring about salvation, hope, and beauty.

And that brave woman is my momma!

Now I see what a great sacrifice she made for me. But as a kid, I never thought to imagine what it would have been like to watch her daughter's first steps and not be able to share it with someone. I never put myself in her shoes to imagine what courage it must have taken to give up her dream of having children in the context of a loving marriage in order to let me live. I didn't understand the profound sacrifices my mom made to put food on the table. Or how she left her wild life to give me stability and love. Or that she was plagued by a feeling of not being good enough for God most of her life.

I wish I could have seen then that MaryAnn was more than just my mom. She was also smart, funny, creative, and loyal. An amazing seamstress and craft connoisseur. The type of woman I'd want to be friends with when I grew up. If I had seen that then, I think it would have changed our relationship.

So let me ask you: Is it possible that there are a couple of interesting, complex, courageous people hiding in plain sight under your roof?

I know it's hard to imagine—trust me, I know!—but your parents actually had lives before you existed. They had dreams and desires and wondered how those things would change once kids came into the picture. If they've never volunteered that information, maybe it's time to ask.

Philippians 2:4 says, "Don't look out only for your own

interests, but take an interest in others, too." Here are a few ideas to do just that:

- Ask your parents questions—lots of them! Ask about their childhoods, their teen years, and even what it's like to be a parent today. To get you started, you'll find a list of questions on pages 212–213.

- If you don't feel comfortable talking one-on-one or you want to remember their answers forever, a memory journal makes a great Christmas, birthday, or Mother's/Father's Day gift. You can find a list of my favorites at www.LifeLoveandGod.com/family.

- Ask your mom or dad if you can go on a "blind date"—just the two of you. While you're out together, imagine it really is your first date and you don't know anything about each other. Allow your perceptions of Mom or Dad to change as you get to know her or him for the "first" time, and encourage your parent to do the same for you.

The Truth about Parenting

After Paul and I had been married a few years, I got the baby bug pretty bad. I'd daydream about what it would be like to have a child of my own: a little person who shared my DNA. A baby I could hold, feed, and dress in all those adorable little itsy-bitsy clothes I saw at the mall. (I mean, really, why does everything look so cute in miniature?) I dreamed of decorating a baby room, cuddling before bedtime, slobbery kisses, and baby's first words. I longed to be Momma to a sweet little thing whom I could shower with love and attention and carry in one of those trendy baby carriers (the leather handbag of the mommy world)—someone who would love me in return. I knew parenting wouldn't be all sugar and spice, but I somehow romanticized even the challenges I heard other parents talk about, like diapers, and late nights, and little temper tantrums.

When I found out I was pregnant with our first daughter, Ryan Kailey, I stocked up on cuter-than-life onesies and thumbed religiously through Pottery Barn Kids magazines. I read *What to Expect When You're Expecting*, lubed my belly with anti–stretch mark oils, and made spreadsheets (yes, spreadsheets—don't judge) comparing strollers and cribs. I thought I was ready. And I was . . . for the *delivery*. But there was no way to actually prepare for the *parenting* part. The idea of having a cute little baby is one thing, but actually having your world turned upside down by the huge task of shaping a person's life when you feel completely inadequate is entirely different.

Parenting is hard.

Before I had my two girls—whom I love with all my heart, by the way—I could get up when I wanted to, eat when I felt like it, take a bike ride if I had a whim, and plan getaways with my husband whenever we wanted. Parenting limits your freedom. It's also the most humbling task I've ever undertaken. I, Jessie Minassian—a confident, educated, self-respecting woman—have been the object of eye rolling, foot stomping, and all manner of disregard from two pint-sized humans. Parenting teaches you that you are nowhere near as competent, calm, or cool as you thought you were.

I've read a dozen parenting books, prayed to high heaven for wisdom, and ~~interrogated~~ interviewed every "good" parent I've met. And yet some days (make that *most* days) I don't have a clue what I'm doing.

Like I said, parenting is hard.

But I embrace the challenge (while simultaneously praying that God will fix all the things I mess up and/or help me afford the counseling bill my kids will send me someday).

The parents in your life have embraced the challenge too.

When they first found out there was a baby on the way, I bet they were filled with equal parts awe and terror. And for good reason! Being solely responsible for the care of a helpless little life is not something to take lightly. And navigating the road between birth and adulthood isn't a walk in the park either.

If parents tackle parenting God's way, they're responsible for

- training their daughter through loving discipline (Proverbs 23:13-14; Ephesians 6:4);
- guiding her through the land mines of life (1 Corinthians 4:14);
- providing for her needs without spoiling her (2 Corinthians 12:14);
- protecting her from herself and others (Matthew 18:12-14); and

- teaching and encouraging godliness (Deuteronomy 6:6-7).

Parents have to *learn* how to do those things; it sure as snot doesn't come naturally! Moms and dads are still sinful, selfish humans in need of God's grace. And most of us are still working through our own baggage. Let's talk about that next.

Parents Have Baggage Too

Parents have hopes and dreams, just like you do. They've sacrificed a lot to be parents, and deep down they want to do it right, even though at times they mess up royally. But parents also have baggage. And understanding our parents' childhoods, cultural upbringings, hurts, and fears can help us see them, and why they do what they do, in new ways.

Remember that time I wanted to run away? In the universe I lived in (the one where everyone and everything else orbited around me), it felt like my world was caving in on itself. At the core of the drama going on in my heart was a troubled relationship with my stepdad. At the time I was stuffing my JanSport, things between him and me were tense, to put it mildly. He seemed angry and unreasonable a lot. I didn't like the way he parented, and I hated how much he and my mom fought. From my perspective, he felt like the root of a lot of my problems—problems that were rocking me to the core.

But if it had been *Freaky Friday* and I'd been forced to switch places with him for a week or two, I would have seen the situation from a completely different angle. At that time, Dad had been out of work for nearly a year, a really stressful thing for a man trying to support a family. He was also trying to work on a marriage that wasn't easy for either of them, and he battled his own fears of failure and not being good enough. Plus, growing up he hadn't had a very good example of parenting. He was the third generation in a line of men who were hot-tempered and verbally and physically abusive. He wanted the cycle to end with him, but as a new Christian, he was still figuring out how to ditch those habits and live God's way.

Dad was broken.

But you know what? We all are.

We all have our weaknesses—those flaws in our characters that we (hopefully) spend our whole lives learning to overcome through the power of the Holy Spirit. And whether we like it or not, most of us have experiences and emotions from our childhoods that shape us well into adulthood. I didn't know then just how much of my dad's temper and anger issues were learned from his dad, who had learned it from his dad, and so on. If I had, I might have felt more compassion for him. I might have recognized how far he had come in taming his outbursts. I might have spent more time praying for him and less time resenting him.

If I could have seen our relationship from his perspective, I also would have had another aha moment: *He didn't* have to *love me.*

Remember the story I told earlier in this chapter about how my mom found out she was pregnant and decided to raise me on her own, as a single mom? Well, a few years into it, a man named Arthur gave her a ring and said with his signature humor, "Put it on if you want to." (Classic proposal, right?) My mom did put it on, and I was five years old when they tied the knot. With the marriage, he acquired a "cute but precocious" (as he remembers) kindergartener who, in his opinion, needed a good dose of discipline. But he chose to take me on. *He chose to call me his.*

He called me daughter.

He fed me and clothed me.

He went to a gazillion of my sporting events.

He let me borrow his favorite sweatshirt (like every time it came out of the wash).

He told me he was proud of me.

This was completely lost on me as a teenager. I didn't have much recollection of our first few years together as a blended family, and—because I was the center of my universe, remember—I suppose I assumed that everyone *must* love me unconditionally. It never occurred to me that he *chose* unconditional love for me. Even though I wasn't his. Even though I wasn't always easy to love.

My dad and I have a very different relationship now: warm and caring. It's painful for both of us to remember that time of stress and misunderstanding. (By the way, kudos to him and his humility for not only letting his failures be put in print but also allowing *someone else* to do the storytelling.) He and I agreed to share this story because when we begin to view our parents as human beings—men and women with fears, faults, and even baggage—we begin to see things about them we can be thankful for. And that's when we're in a good position to show our parents God's grace. The same grace we've been given. The kind of grace that turns haters into lovers, and sinners into saints. God's grace covers *every* sin and is for *every* one of us who loves Him. Without it, you and I would both be in bad shape. Same with your parents.

And if your parents don't have a relationship with God, you can show grace there, too! Can you imagine how hard it is to go through life without the forgiveness, wisdom, and hope God offers? I encourage you to pray for your unsaved parents and, in the meantime, try not to hold them to a standard of holiness they can't reach without Christ at work in their lives. There are some changes people can make only with the help of the Holy Spirit!

So think about your family. Are you having a hard time with some of your parents' tactics? Do you wonder why they do what they do or how they got the way they are? If so, ask God to open your eyes to see them from a new perspective: as fellow journeyers on this path of growing to be more like Christ. Then ask yourself these questions:

- What difficulties have my mom and dad had to overcome in life?
- What sacrifices did they make in order to become parents?
- What sacrifices have my parents made to give me the best life possible?

- How can I show my mom and dad the same grace God has shown me regarding my faults?

I hope this chapter has given you a deeper appreciation for your parents as you've looked at their roles, responsibilities, and lives in a new way. Your newfound knowledge might not change the world before sundown, but hopefully in the coming days and weeks, your fresh appreciation for them will seep into the way you interact. I tell you what: There isn't a parent in the world who has an easy time of it! But as kids, we can make parenthood more of a joy for them by expressing appreciation where appreciation is due and showing respect for our moms and dads for the unique *people* they are, flaws and all. That's just what Christ would want, right? For us to add empathy, grace, and gratitude to that foundation we're building as we allow our family life to make us more like Him.

Father, thank You for giving me my parents. I know they're not perfect. I also know that You love them just as much as You love me and that You're writing their life stories in ways I'll never completely understand this side of heaven. Help me appreciate their humanness in a new way, and give me strength to be gracious in how I treat them. Love You, God. Amen.

Application Questions

1. Have you ever talked to your parents about what life was like for them before they had you? If not, plan a time to do so. Remember, you can use the bonus "Question Time: Getting to Know Your Parents" on pages 211–213 as a guide.

2. *If you have kids someday, do you think you'll share a lot of details about what your life was like before they came into the picture? Why or why not?*

3. *When you think about the possibility of being a mom someday, what scares, excites, and worries you?*

4. *What can you do (or stop doing) as a daughter to help your parents be the best parents they can be?*

5. *Look again at this list of questions. This time write the answers in your journal.*

  • *What difficulties have my mom and dad had to overcome in life?*

  • *What sacrifices did they make in order to become parents?*

  • *What sacrifices have my parents made to give me the best life possible?*

  • *How can I show my mom and dad the same grace God has shown me regarding my faults?*

CHAPTER THREE

Ouch! (Learning to Forgive)

I HATE PAIN. In fact, I go to great lengths to avoid it. For example, after one excruciating attempt at waxing my bikini area, I have hitherto sworn to N-E-V-E-R again get within two feet of my lady parts with wax. Ever. Yeah, I know it's "soooo convenient" in swimsuit season. Whatever. I can barely handle pulling a Band-Aid off my skin, let alone the heart-attack-producing pain of a bikini wax. Some might call me a baby, but I prefer to think of myself as having the gift of heightened sensory perception. (That should be a scientific term. If it's not, I claim myself the discoverer of said gifting and own it proudly.) I am so sensitive to pain that I even get sympathy pains in my back when I see someone *else* in pain.

Is that weird? My daughter shows me a splinter and I feel it right in the small of my back. I know—I'm special. But even if you don't have HSP (see what I did there?), I doubt you like pain either. In fact, I've never met anyone who likes to get hurt. Most of us avoid it like last decade's fashion fads. Unfortunately for you and me, everyone will experience pain in life, and that pain, by definition, hurts!

As much we dislike physical pain, emotional pain is worse, isn't it? There will be times when our carefully planned lives flip like pancakes, moments when our feelings get run over by a semi, circumstances when people let us down (*way* down). And there's no question that the more we love the people who hurt us, *the more it hurts.* That's why family hurts cut so deeply.

I wish I could grab a couple of iced favorites and invite you to hang out with me today to talk about your family life and the ways you've been hurt and the frustrations you're facing. I know your family's junk is different from mine, and I wish I knew exactly how you've been hurt through your family and how you've handled that hurt. Maybe your birth mom gave you up for adoption. Maybe your dad is so busy with work that he doesn't seem to have time for you or he says things that cut you to the core. Maybe you lost your favorite grandma to cancer. Maybe your big brother is putting stress on the family with his rebellious antics or you have a sister whose goal in life seems to be hurting your feelings. I don't know if you've been abused, neglected, put on a pedestal, or teased, but I do know that every single one of us has been hurt by our family in some way.

Every. Single. One.

Every family since sin's debut in the Garden of Eden has been affected by sin. Damaged by it. Confused by it. Hurt by it. Broken by it. That's why one of the first things we have to apply to that foundation we talked about is forgiveness. We need to know what forgiveness is—and just as important, what it *isn't*—if we're going to grow to be more like Jesus.

What's Forgiveness?

Forgiveness is a huge topic, and I can't do it justice in the few pages we have here. So consider this the CliffsNotes version of a big faith topic that you'll spend your whole life studying and refining. My goal is to make you crave more, like offering you one bite of a triple-fudge brownie (cruel—that's just *cruel*).

If I had to boil down the big topic of forgiveness into one sentence, it would be this: *Forgiveness is giving up your right to hold a sin against, or expect repayment from, a person who hurt you.*

See, when we've been wronged, what we really want is for the other person to somehow pay for what he or she did. We want to see the person who hurt us suffer as we did or at the very least feel painfully guilty. And under the Old Covenant God had with His chosen people (the Israelites), that's pretty much how it worked. If someone broke your cart or plow, he or she had to dish out the money to replace your cart or plow. If someone broke your leg, guess who'd be walking with a limp? If someone killed your ox, you had every right to take his or hers. In our human minds this makes total sense, doesn't it? I should get back what I lost from the person who took it from me. That feels *fair*.

But when Jesus came to earth, He blew *fair* right out of the water. He taught radical—seriously *nuts*—ideas, like this one:

> You have heard the law that says the punishment
> must match the injury: "An eye for an eye, and a
> tooth for a tooth." But I say, do not resist an evil
> person! If someone slaps you on the right cheek,
> offer the other cheek also. If you are sued in court
> and your shirt is taken from you, give your coat, too.
>
> MATTHEW 5:38-40

The people listening to Jesus must have thought He had been turning water into wine again, if you know what I mean. I can hear the murmur rippling through the crowd: "Did you hear what Jesus just said? That's insane!" The idea of giving up your right to get revenge from someone who hurts you was (and is) crazy talk. Who would *do* that? I'll tell you who: absolutely no one. And that's exactly why Jesus asks us to do it. What better way to show the world that there is a God than to offer someone forgiveness when it doesn't make sense, it isn't fair, and they certainly don't deserve it?

Recap time: Forgiveness is giving up your right to hold a sin against, or expect repayment from, a person who hurt you. It means giving up your right to "fair" in light of all that God has forgiven you for (see Matthew 6:14-15; Colossians 3:13).

Now let's talk about what forgiveness *isn't*, okay?

Five Forgiveness Myths

A lot of people spend their lives confused about forgiveness. (Maybe because it's so counterintuitive?) I was one of them. But as I grew and learned more about God's Word and His best for my life, I began to see that some of the "truths" I attached to forgiveness were just plain lies. If that's you, too, let's set the record straight about five popular myths.

Myth #1: Forgiveness means you agree with or support the person's actions.

Truth: I can forgive someone even when what he or she did was 100 percent wrong.

Myth #2: Forgiveness makes you a doormat because you can never stand up for yourself.

Truth: Jesus taught that true strength is found in humility (see Matthew 5:5). You can forgive and still set clear boundaries.

Myth #3: If you've really forgiven someone, you won't feel hurt anymore.

Truth: Forgiveness doesn't always erase pain, especially not at first.

Myth #4: It's fine to wait indefinitely for the person to apologize before you forgive him or her.
Truth: You can forgive someone even if he or she never admits to being wrong or apologizes.

Myth #5: Forgiving means forgetting.
Truth: You might never forget what happened, even when you've truly forgiven someone. God is all-knowing, so He's well aware of all the sins we've ever committed, but He has chosen to forgive and not hold them against us.

That last one is so important that I want to dive into it a little deeper. You game?

Peter, one of Jesus' disciples, once asked Jesus just how many times he should forgive someone. See, the Jews had a custom that if someone jacked you seven times in the same way, you could write the person off. You had done your fair share and could now check the little "forgiveness" box on your spiritual task list. But Jesus' answer didn't jive with what Peter had been taught. Let's listen in on the conversation:

> Then Peter came to him and asked, "Lord, how often should I forgive someone who sins against me? Seven times?"
>
> "No, not seven times," Jesus replied, "but seventy times seven!"
>
> MATTHEW 18:21-22

Four hundred ninety times for the same stupid thing done to you? Not only is that radical, but it seems a little unrealistic. I mean, I get the point, Jesus, but I can't think of anyone in my life who has sinned against me *in the same way* that many times. So what did Jesus mean by those words?

The obvious lesson is that we shouldn't put a limit on how many times we forgive someone when he or she sins against us. But Jesus had a divine knack for weaving layers into His teaching, and I have a hunch that might be the case here. What if Jesus also meant that we'd sometimes need to forgive someone up to four hundred ninety times in our hearts for *the same hurtful thing* done to us? In other words, for the same offense? Because forgiving doesn't mean forgetting and because I'm a sinner with a heart bent on whining about fairness, there have definitely been times in my life when a memory of something done to me resurfaces and I have to re-forgive that person in my heart. Again. And again. And one more time for good measure. When I look at forgiveness as a process of letting go of "fair" over and over in my heart, that four hundred ninety times starts looking necessary.

Forgiveness is *not* a Mr. Clean Magic Eraser. Have you seen those things? That white sponge does miracles, I tell you. Got Sharpie on your white desk? Rub-a-dub and presto chango! No more Sharpie. Scuff marks on a floor, or mildew on the shower wall? Gone. Battery acid on an oak floor? See ya. (True story.) There's nothing those little sponges can't get rid of. But forgiveness won't make the hurts magically disappear. And if they don't just disappear, that means the pain sometimes lingers. So what happens when we find ourselves reliving hurts from people we love? How do we deal with the pain?

I can give you no better advice when it comes to family-caused pain (or any pain, for that matter) than this: Hold tight to God. He's the only one who will always know just the right words to say, has the power to give you supernatural peace, and wants to comfort you and grow you, no strings attached. Here are some of the ways God comforted and helped King David when he was at his wit's end:

My father and mother walked out and left me,
> but GOD took me in. . . .
I'm sure now I'll see God's goodness
> in the exuberant earth.
Stay with GOD!
> Take heart. Don't quit.
I'll say it again:
> Stay with GOD.

PSALM 27:10, 13-14, MSG

"If you'll hold on to me for dear life," says GOD,
> "I'll get you out of any trouble.
I'll give you the best of care
> if you'll only get to know and trust me.
Call me and I'll answer, be at your side in bad times;
> I'll rescue you. . . .
I'll give you a long life,
> give you a long drink of salvation!"

PSALM 91:14-16, MSG

Reading those verses just now brought tears to my eyes. What amazing comfort! The God of the universe promises to take care of us, to be by our sides, to rescue us, if only we'll get to know and trust Him. That's our part. If we want to make it through the pain caused by our families, we have to dive headlong into our relationship with our Divine Daddy: our God full of kindness, warmth, and tenderness.

When life delivers the hardest punches, we are usually tempted to turn to people to comfort us: to our friends, to our parents, and especially to guys. I know that. But God is the only one who will always be there for you, sis—who will always have the best advice and purest comfort. Don't take Him for granted!

How to Deal with the Pain

Truly forgiving also includes dealing with our pain in healthy ways. Healing can't take place if we ignore the pain or cope with it in destructive ways, such as cutting, eating disorders, anger, or internalizing our emotions. So let's talk about some healthy ways to deal with hurt.

LET GOD'S WORD ROCK YOU

Hebrews 4:12 tells us that the Word of God is "alive and powerful [and] sharper than the sharpest two-edged sword." It's so sharp that it can cut through any walls we've put up in our hearts, letting God heal us right where we need it. The Bible speaks to our hearts in uncanny ways. Get into it and get refreshed.

When We Hurt Ourselves

When our hearts have been wounded, it's easy to turn to unhelpful, unhealthy stuff to make the pain go away— to feel as if we're in control. If you struggle with an eating disorder, cutting, substance abuse, sexual addiction, or any other "secret sin," I'd love to walk with you on a journey to freedom and healing through my book *Unashamed: Overcoming the Sins No Girl Wants to Talk About.* It's time to break the silence. You are not alone!

TALK TO GOD

A lot of us have this funny habit of praying, "God, show me how to handle such and such situation," saying amen, and then going about life as usual, never giving Him a second thought throughout the day. It's like messaging a friend with "Do you want to hang out this weekend?" but never messaging back to figure out the details, such as when and where to meet. How can God show us how to handle difficult or painful situations if we're not willing to spend time with Him, working out the details? Jesus said, "Come to me . . . and I will give you rest" (Matthew 11:28). Before we can find that rest, we have to come to Him. Talk to Him. Spend time chatting it up about our feelings, experiences, and pain.

EXERCISE

There's nothing like a good run, walk on the beach, dance class, or bike ride to lift a girl's spirits. Not only are you taking care of the body God has given you (which is a very good thing), but the endorphins your body releases are a natural pick-me-up. For extra credit, you can use your time alone as you run, walk, ride, or swim to talk with God about your feelings.

WRITE

Studies have shown that people who write about their feelings tend to have a better handle on them. Whether you keep a journal, write poetry, blog, or create music, writing forces you to sift through your feelings to get to the root causes of them.

I'll be honest—sometimes a good old-fashioned, dark and depressing venting session is in order. *However*, if you stay there forever, you're going to drown in your own depressing puddles of words. It's okay to write about your sadness or hurt. King David (writer of many a psalm) wasn't shy about his pain, anger, and amped-up desire for justice. But in the end, his psalms almost always circled back around to God's love, truth, and victory. He didn't stay in the dregs forever; he remembered hope. And infusing *your* writing with hope will do wonders for your heart.

TALK WITH A FRIEND

I know that finding a friend who will listen and has wise advice can be about as hard to find as genuine Uggs at Goodwill. But look for one. And if you find one, confide in her. The proverb is true that "some friends don't help, but a true friend is closer than your own family" (Proverbs 18:24, CEV). A true friend can help you see aspects of a situation you hadn't thought of, pray for you when you're stuck, and bring joy and companionship to the hard days.

LOOK OUTSIDE YOURSELF

Your family life might stink. Genuinely. But if you focus on only your own misery, you'll miss opportunities to be a friend to others, serve selflessly, love deeply, and represent Christ to your friends and family. There's a whole world out there that needs the love of Christ, and you can offer it. Don't let Satan sideline you from this huge spiritual battle we're in by convincing you that you can't fight when you're in pain. Even those gifted with "heightened sensory perception" (aka pain wimps) like I am can cowgirl up and fight through life's hurts.

A Picture of Forgiveness

There's a story in the Old Testament that puts flesh and bones on everything we've been talking about. It's a story you've likely heard since your head barely reached the top of my knee-high leather boots (favorite shoes in my closet, if you care to know). Please don't let the familiarity of this story ruin the huge application it can hold for us. Deal?

Back in the day (way back), Joseph was his dad's favorite son. His brothers were more than a tad bit jealous of their little brother for getting all Dad's attention. (I can't say I blame them for that part.) But Joey's older brothers let their jealousy consume them, and eventually they were so ticked about it that they sold their little brother into slavery to get

him out of their hair. For two decades, Joseph felt the consequences of their actions. He worked as a slave for a while,
before he was thrown into prison for something he didn't do.
Then, through a series of events that the best novelists can
only imitate, Joseph became second-in-command throughout
the land of Egypt during a big famine. The famine brought
Joseph's brothers on a quest to find food, and they ended up
on his new home turf, with their faces in the dirt in front of
him. They were completely vulnerable, and in that moment,
Joseph had the power to take whatever revenge he wanted.

Time-out. Now, if you were Joseph, wouldn't you be
tempted to throw those bros into the same dungeon that you
had done time in? I mean, Joseph suffered T-W-E-N-T-Y
years because of them! I can't say that I would have shown
mercy. But (granted, after a prank that scared the jujubes out
of his brothers) Joseph's response was insanely noble: "You
intended to harm me, but God intended it all for good"
(Genesis 50:20). Then he gave his brothers food and all sorts
of good things and asked them to come live with him in
Egypt.

Say what!

Wow. That's the perfect picture of forgiveness: having the
ability to pay someone back for all the hurt he or she has caused
you and instead offering blessing. And like a bonus purse and
cosmetics during "gift time" at your favorite makeup counter,
when you offer forgiveness instead of resentment or revenge,
you take home something unexpected: *healing*.

Win-win.

The Gift of Pain

Remember the secret? God wants to use every hurt in our lives—whether from a breakup or our family stuff—to make us more like Jesus. Even if the source of our pain isn't our fault and/or breaks God's heart (see "What about Abuse?" on page 14), we can still learn from the experience. James put it this way:

> Consider it a sheer gift, friends, when tests and challenges come at you from all sides. You know that under pressure, your faith-life is forced into the open and shows its true colors. So don't try to get out of anything prematurely. Let it do its work so you become mature and well-developed, not deficient in any way.
>
> JAMES 1:2-4, MSG

That's pretty challenging stuff, isn't it? I don't know about you, but when someone cuts me deep, my first instinct is to get the heck out of there. To make the pain stop! And in some cases, this is an appropriate and right response. But James tells us that most run-of-the-mill hard times are opportunities to see what our faith is really made of.

If our faith is weak, our entire world will crumble when family members hurt us. But if we allow God to make our hearts stronger—to build us up through the painful words and circumstances we face—we'll come out on the other side a more "mature and well-developed" girl. That's pretty awesome.

So how about it? Will you stand with me and receive every disappointment, pain, worry, and unfairness with both your hands? Will you see your hurts not as God's punishment but as rare opportunities to have a more complete relationship with Jesus, who also suffered much at the hands of others? If you do see your pain in that way, every trial and pressure you face will become the source of your success.

No matter how badly your family members have hurt you, you can say with King David,

> Taste and see that the LORD is good.
>> Oh, the joys of those who take refuge
>>> in him! . . .
> The LORD is close to the brokenhearted;
>> he rescues those whose spirits are crushed.
> PSALM 34:8, 18

Should we ask God to help us get there?

Daddy, I am so thankful that You have made me Your daughter. I know that one day I'll get to live with You in person and won't have to worry about pain and suffering, but for now, sometimes life really hurts! Help me find healthy ways to deal with the pain my human family has caused me, and help me forgive them. And show me where I need to ask for forgiveness too. I want to taste the good life that comes when I'm hanging on to You, God, instead of my pain. I love You! Amen.

Application Questions

1. *Have you been hurt in any of these ways by someone in your family?*

   ☐ *Abandonment (by a parent or sibling)*

   ☐ *Abuse (physical, sexual, emotional)*

   ☐ *Alcohol or drug abuse*

   ☐ *Anger or explosiveness*

   ☐ *Break of trust*

   ☐ *Death of a loved one*

   ☐ *Divorce or separation*

   ☐ *Hurtful words*

   ☐ *Lack of love and affection*

   ☐ *Neglect*

   ☐ *Parent's sin (lies, unfaithfulness, breaking the law, and so on)*

   ☐ *Sibling's sin (partying, sex outside of marriage, and so on)*

   ☐ *Other:*

   ☐ *Other:*

2. *Think about the ways your family members have hurt you. Have you forgiven them for what they've done?*

(Remember, forgiving does not usually equal forgetting, but it does mean you've given up holding a grudge or hoping for revenge.)

3. *When someone in your family hurts you, how do you usually cope with the pain you feel?*

4. *When life hurts most, do you turn to God or to other people? How can turning to other people, especially to guys, be dangerous?*

5. *Look back at the healthy ways to cope with pain on pages 47–50. Which do you do already? Which do you want to try?*

6. *If you know in your heart that you haven't completely forgiven the people who have hurt you, write a prayer to God in this space or in your journal, telling Him how you feel and asking Him to show you how to truly forgive.*

CHAPTER FOUR

Ditching the Attitude

"DON'T GIVE ME that attitude!"

Ah, the words I heard five zillion times growing up. They ring like the official anthem of my teen years. There's no way I could remember all the times I got punished, yelled at, or lectured for my attitude. There are way too many to count. But I do remember one incident as though it happened last Tuesday.

It was just a normal weeknight. We were all gathered around the kitchen table for dinner, enjoying a nice meal and getting along fairly well (which was somewhat rare and not to be taken for granted). But the peace was not to last. I don't remember why, but Dad told me to put the milk back in the fridge. Maybe it had been sitting out awhile or something. I'm also not sure why this was such a big deal to me. Maybe Dad got it out in the first place and I felt *he* should be the one to make the long journey—all of ten feet—to the refrigerator. Whatever the reason, I responded in first-class disrespect. First, I slumped my shoulders and rolled my eyes. If he noticed, he didn't let on. Not getting called on it gave me the courage to ratchet up my witchiness. I grabbed the gallon of milk, stomped over to the fridge, swung it open, and before I even really knew what I was doing or why I was doing it, mumbled a four-letter word just quietly enough that I didn't think anyone would hear. But someone did hear. The very last person I wanted to hear.

As I opened the fridge, I heard Dad's low, you'd-better-hope-I'm-wrong voice (resembling a low growl).

"*What* did you say?"

My mind raced. *Oh, I am sooo dead. Seriously, my life is about to end.* I tried not to let him see me sweat. I mustered every ounce of believability and pushed out the word.

"Nothing."

To this day, I don't know why I didn't get grounded for the remainder of my life at that moment. Dad was not one to trifle with. Maybe he wasn't completely sure I said what he thought he heard me say. Whatever the reasons, he let it slide.

But that was just the beginning of *my* slide. Early in my teen years, I hit a turning point in my attitude. My mood toward my family became like a game of Chutes and Ladders, except there were way more slides down than heroic climbs up. Can you relate?

Deep down there was always this little whisper that let me know when my attitude was out of line, but no teenager admits to that. It's against an adolescent code or something. So I had to become a master of two things: (1) faking my innocence, and (2) justifying my position. I learned to convince myself that whatever attitude I was flinging at my parents or siblings was, well, *deserved.* If Dad told me to take out the trash, I'd defend my huff-and-stuff with thoughts like, *Well, if he had asked me a little more nicely, it wouldn't be such a big deal. He's so mean!* Or if I got home from school and Mom told me to do my homework before going to a friend's house, I'd roll my eyes and wonder, *Why doesn't she just trust me? It's not like I get bad grades or anything.* As for my brothers and sister, I never really felt I needed to justify my attitude toward them. How's that for delusional?

I guess I feel safe sharing my me-centeredness with you because I know I'm not alone. In fact, when I asked teen girls what they argue about most with their parents, "attitude" made the short list. Big surprise.

In our teen years, we face an explosive combo of (1) needing to become our own people, (2) our parents learning to *let* us be our own people, (3) plain old sin in our hearts, and (4) a hormone-juiced monthly cycle. And when you put those fearsome things together, my friend, it can be really hard to honor our parents, if you know what I mean. We can find ourselves being sassy, arrogant, passive-aggressive, snippy, and just downright *mean*, almost against our wills.

I found it so frustrating to *want* to ditch my bad attitude but not know where to start. So I just sort of embraced it as inevitable. I'm convinced that a lot of girls feel that. So in this chapter, I want to give you the reasons why a good attitude is, well, *good* and some practical tips to make an effort at civility with your family. I can't promise to fix it all because I don't think there *is* a perfect solution (apart from heaven) to that otherworldly concoction of independence, sin, and hormones. But I do know that with the help of God's Spirit, we can "put to death the sinful, earthly things lurking within [us]" (Colossians 3:5) and learn to see the struggle to rein in our attitude as yet another way we can become more like Jesus Christ. Bonus: Working on our attitudes is one of the best ways to help our families like us back.

The Fifth Commandment

When God brought His children, the Israelites, out of Egypt, He wanted to give them some guidelines for how to live life the best possible way. So He called Moses up to Mount Sinai and told him to listen carefully as He gave him His "Top Ten" list of rules (what we now call the Ten Commandments). The first four rules God gave described how we should treat Him: God should be first in our lives; we should worship Him and set aside time to be with Him. Then He changed His focus, and the rest of the rules explain how we should treat other people. Interestingly enough, the very first one of those others-focused rules—the fifth commandment—describes how kids should treat their parents. Here's what it says: "Honor your father and mother. Then you will live a long, full life in the land the LORD your God is giving you" (Exodus 20:12).

I'll tell you this: There was a time in my life when this verse offered very little motivation to honor my parental unit. If the promised reward for honoring Mom and Pop was that I'd get to live longer on earth—with *them*—well, that was not exactly inspirational. I would rather have died young—*very* young.

But let's back up. Is it just me, or is it odd that God started out the relational commandments with this one? If it had been my show, I probably would have started out with the biggies, like "Don't murder" and "Don't commit adultery" (see Exodus 20:13-14), just to make sure Moses knew I meant business. Those commands more clearly justify the "flashes of lightning" and the "smoke billowing from the mountain" (see verse 18) that was going on, don't you think? But before God talked about my top choices—*or* about lying, stealing, and jealousy—He told us to honor our parents. That makes me wonder, *Why is honoring them so important to God?*

Because I'm not God—surprise, surprise—I can't know for sure. I do, however, have a hunch.

I think God cares so much about kids honoring their parents because it's our training ground.

Honoring our parents is the way we learn to honor God Himself.

Think about it. God just spent four commandments telling His people to honor Him. But a child isn't born into this world automatically knowing how to do that. In fact, our sin nature makes the opposite true: We're born rebels. Because we're broken, fallen people, we have to *learn how* to honor. We have to *practice* submission. We have to *train* in the fine art of respecting authority. Left to ourselves, we don't want to bend our selfish will to anyone or anything.

Enter our parents: the perfect scenario for learning how to honor people even when we don't understand their reasons, agree with their methods, or appreciate their consequences. *Especially then.*

If we can get a handle on those skills while under our parents' roofs, we'll have inadvertently learned how to honor, submit to, and respect God's authority, even when we don't understand, agree with, or appreciate His methods.

Pretty deep, right? When we understand honoring our parents that way, ditching our bad attitudes becomes a holy experience. Learning to obey without an eye roll becomes part of growing to be more like Jesus—which, as we've already seen, is what all of life is about.

Another Case for Honor

Now let's fast-forward through the Bible a couple of thousand years.

The apostle Paul referred to the fifth commandment while teaching his Ephesian friends. He knew that sometimes it's hard to know how those relational commands should look in the practical, day-to-day of life. So Paul addressed some of the most common relationships and how we can honor Christ and put others first in each one. This one should sound familiar:

> Children, obey your parents because you belong
> to the Lord, for this is the right thing to do.
> "Honor your father and mother." This is the first
> commandment with a promise: If you honor your
> father and mother, "things will go well for you, and
> you will have a long life on the earth."
>
> EPHESIANS 6:1-3

This little passage has more guts to dissect than a frog. Are you ready?

First, Paul reminds us that the whole reason we're to honor our parents (by obeying—hold that thought) is because *we belong to the Lord*. This is huge, as it means honoring our parents doesn't depend on their worthiness.

God has bought each believer with the blood of His Son, Jesus (see 1 Corinthians 6:19-20). Personally, I think we got the *way* better end of the bargain on this one. Let's see . . . we were completely dead to sin and had absolutely nothing going for us, and then God came and offered us life, identity, and purpose—and it didn't cost us a single dollar. All we have to do is admit we are miserable sinners without Christ (check), believe that Jesus died as payment for *our* sin (check), and ask Him to save our pitiful little tushies from ourselves so we can live life for Him (and check). Yup, we pretty much got the sweetest deal of all recorded time.

In response to that better-than-Black-Friday deal, "belonging to the Lord"—and therefore honoring our folks—is a joyful "get to" instead of a forced "have to." It's possible to be so excited about our adoption into God's family that we want to do *everything* He asks us to do because we're so full of love for Him.

So we honor our parents because we belong to the Lord. But we're not done with these verses yet! Read them one more time, paying special attention to how Paul uses the words *honor* and *obey*.

> Children, *obey* your parents because you belong
> to the Lord, for this is the right thing to do.
> "*Honor* your father and mother." This is the first
> commandment with a promise: If you *honor* your
> father and mother, "things will go well for you, and
> you will have a long life on the earth" (emphasis
> added).

He seems to use the two words interchangeably, right? Here are their English definitions:

honor ('ä-nər) *verb*—to regard or treat with honor or respect[1]

obey (ō-'bā) *verb*—1: to follow the commands or guidance of; 2: to conform to or comply with[2]

Here's where it gets really good—or really scary, depending on which side of the parent-child relationship you're sitting on. If we look at our parents and understand that they are worth our respect (i.e., honor), if only because God has handpicked them to be our parents, we'll follow their instructions and listen to their advice (i.e., obey). (Unless your parents tell you to do something—or do something to you—that goes against God's Word. God's laws trump parents' instructions every time.)

Once our attitudes are in the right place, our actions will almost always follow suit. But is it possible to honor God by obeying our parents even when we don't *feel* like it—I mean *really* don't feel like it? Check out this story and see what you think.

A TALE OF TWO DAUGHTERS

Once upon a time, a man named Eric had two daughters, Amanda and Ashlyn. Every summer the girls helped out on the family ranch to earn a little extra spending money for the school year. At breakfast one mid-July day, Eric told his youngest daughter, Ashlyn, he wanted her to clean out the horses' stalls before dinner. She smiled and said, "Okay, Daddy," and then went back to devouring her blueberry pancakes.

Then Eric asked Amanda to weed her mom's vegetable garden before dinner. Amanda wrinkled her nose and slumped down into her chair. "Why do you always give me the hardest jobs? Ashlyn always gets off easier. Anyway, I can't today because I already made plans."

When Ashlyn finished her pancakes, she got

distracted on her phone, and by the afternoon it was so hot that she decided to go swimming with her friends instead of taking care of the horse stalls. But when Amanda finished her breakfast, she got to thinking. Even though she really wanted to hang with her friends, she realized that listening to her dad was the right thing to do. She was none too happy when she texted her friends to say she couldn't hang out, but she grabbed her Beats and headed out to the garden for a hard day's work.

Which daughter obeyed her dad? Ashlyn or Amanda?

Even though Amanda had a bad attitude at first, she ended up doing what her dad asked of her.

Does the story sound familiar? It's actually a modern-day version of a parable Jesus told (you can read it in Matthew 21:28-31). Jesus' point was that regardless of how we start out, God cares most about how we finish. That's really good news for those of us still figuring out the honoring part of "Honor and obey"! I wish I always had the perfect attitude when I'm told to do something, but I fail just about as often as I succeed. Still. Sadly. Yet according to Jesus, if I do what I'm supposed to do, even though I'm still working on the honoring bit, God's still counts my obedience. And He *really* wants my obedience. In Proverbs 3:1-2, Solomon says, "My child, remember my teachings and instructions and obey them completely. They will help you live a long and prosperous life" (CEV).

Of course, having a good attitude on top of obedience

is best, not just for the people we live with but also for ourselves. A rotten attitude just makes *us* miserable while we have to do whatever it is we have to do (or don't do what we're not allowed to do). But if we can muster a good attitude, the chore, rule, or consequence our parents give us usually isn't nearly as bad as we thought it would be. Am I right?

To review, if honoring is an attitude, obedience is the resulting action. Obedience puts hands and feet on your honoring. But what happens when you *still* can't seem to get the honoring part down? Even though you want to? Here come those practical tips I promised (and this part might be as much for me as for you!).

Four Tips for Troubleshooting Your 'Tude

Tip #1: Check Your Heart

One little word in one little proverb speaks volumes about the how-to in ditching attitude: "Children who curse their parents will go to the land of darkness long before their time" (Proverbs 20:20, CEV).

I know, it doesn't mention attitude at all. And you might read that verse and think (like I did), *Well, then it's a good thing I don't cuss out my parents. Man, who would do that, anyway?* But when we look at the Hebrew word translated *curse* in Proverbs 20:20 (CEV), we find that we're not off the hook. The word is *kawlal*,[3] and it doesn't limit cursing to bad words or witches' spells. Kawlal can also mean to make light of, to lightly esteem, or to despise. Anyone out there ever made light of her parents' authority? (Please tell me I'm not the only one.) How about ignored their rules? Or looked down on them for "not understanding" or being "so uncool"? You could think of kawlal as an epic eye roll.

Gut-check time: Disrespect for our parents can be as simple as not thinking of them as God does or hating them (if even for a moment) in our hearts. It might show itself in something as "small" as our body language or as "big" as an all-out verbal fistfight, but to God it's all the same.

Here's the practical takeaway from Proverbs 20:20: If we really want to change our attitudes toward our parents, we have to genuinely believe, deep down in our hearts (not just with our words), that they are *worth* our honor. And this is not only if they're fair, wise, kind, patient, understanding, and cool—because they might not be. In fact, they probably *won't* be, at least not all of the time. No, they are worth your honor because God has given them a position of authority over you for this season of your life. It's hard for me to even type those words because I know—man, do I know!—how hard this is to swallow. But our insides (hearts) have to change before our outsides (attitudes) will follow suit.

Luke 6:45 says, "What you say flows from what is in your heart." So if our attitudes stink, we can trace that foul smell right down to our hearts. Get our hearts in the right place, and then our body language, words, and all that good stuff will come up roses.

So tip number one for ditching attitude is to check your heart. Ask yourself if you really honor your parents. And if not, ask God to help you pump out the sewage.

Tip #2: Imagine Your Body Language on Someone Else

My second tip to ditch a bad attitude is to picture someone else using your body language and then try to imagine how it would make you feel. Let's take the eye roll, for example. It's an art form, really. In one little motion, with two little body parts, we can say any number of things:

- Whatever.
- I don't give a rip what you think.
- I think your rules are stupid.
- You're so unfair.
- I've heard all this before—stop lecturing me.
- The nineties called. It wants its clothes back.
- I know that what you're saying is true, but I don't want to hear it.
- Stop treating me like I'm five.

An eye roll gets our feelings across, all right. But how would you feel if someone you cared about rolled his or her eyes in disgust or irritation at you? Not exactly going to foster nice feelings, agreed? The same goes for slumped shoulders, stomping, slamming, and the silent treatment. Oh, and hiding behind headphones. Not that any of us has ever done that, right? Imagining our body language on someone else helps us see how ugly our attitudes really are.

Tip #3: Listen to Your Voice

It's easy to get lazy in the way we talk to our parents (or even our siblings). It's all so familiar, and that makes it easy to slip into negative habits. I know this probably sounds weird and maybe even a little ridiculous, but I *promise* you it works! The next time you're around your parents in a situation where you usually end up having trouble communicating with each other civilly, try recording your voice during the conversation. Most phones have a voice-memo feature (or you could download an app). Play it back to yourself later on and take note of your word choices, volume, phrases, and tone of voice. You might be surprised to hear what your family hears! When I tried this, I was amazed how different my words sounded compared with how I *thought* they sounded. Humiliating? Possibly. But also helpful, if we're teachable.

I do remember times when my parents would accuse me of attitude and I'd genuinely feel innocent of the charges. I think sometimes we experts in the art of giving attitude don't even *realize* when we're doing it anymore. If you're in that spot, genuinely not knowing why your parents think you give them attitude, this final tip is for you.

Tip #4: Ask Your Parents for Feedback

Sit down with your parents and ask them to tell you specific ways they see you show disrespect. Huge disclaimer here: If you do this, you're probably going to want to tell them a hundred reasons why they're misunderstanding you, delusional, or just plain out of their minds. Fight the urge! Accept what they say in humility, and then spend some time alone with God asking Him if your parents could be right, if even just a little teensy bit. Proverbs 12:1 has to be your prayer for this tip to work: "If you love learning, you love the discipline that goes with it—how shortsighted to refuse correction!" (MSG).

So those are my four tips for troubleshooting your attitude when you really want to change but aren't sure where to start. And here they are as a quick-reference checklist. Stick a paper clip on this page so you can refer back to it when you feel stuck in a bad-attitude black hole.

Jessie's Attitude Troubleshooting List

☐ *Check Your Heart*
   Ask, *Do I really respect my parents right now, or does my attitude reek of sewage in my heart?*

☐ *Imagine Your Body Language on Someone Else*
   Ask, *If my best friend gave me nonverbal cues like this, how would I feel?*

☐ *Listen to Your Voice*
   Use your phone to record a conversation with your parents. Play it back and listen objectively to how you sound. Are you representing yourself the way you want to come across?

☐ *Ask Your Parents for Feedback*
Ask your parents to explain ways they think your attitude needs to change. Remember to listen graciously and with a big dose of humility!

Having a bad attitude toward our parents is just a symptom of a deeper issue: not allowing God to control our lives. When the Holy Spirit is in control of our hearts, He produces qualities like patience, kindness, and the ability to control our emotions. (In chapter 8, we'll talk more about responding the right way when we feel we've been treated unfairly.) It can be a hard pill to swallow, especially when we feel that our parents are *mostly* responsible for the tension. But remember that God will deal with your parents in His own way and in His own time if they are truly in the wrong. That's not your place. Your place is to honor and respect them (even when you are 99.9999 percent sure they are wrong). When you do, God has good things He wants to give you in return for being obedient to Him.

Like Flowers in Your Hair

Having the right attitude and acting in obedience are some of the most beautiful accessories a girl can wear. I love the way this verse in Proverbs describes what it looks like when a girl accepts her parents' counsel with a good attitude:

Pay close attention, friend, to what your father tells you;
never forget what you learned at your mother's knee.

Wear their counsel like flowers in your hair,
 like rings on your fingers.

PROVERBS 1:8-9, MSG (EMPHASIS ADDED)

There aren't many things that show a girl's carefree love of life like fresh-picked wildflowers in her hair. The picture screams sunshine, freedom, and hope. This is where we get back to the promise attached to the fifth commandment. Remember Ephesians 6:1-3? "The first commandment with a promise says, 'Obey your father and your mother, *and you will have a long and happy life*'" (CEV, emphasis added). I thought honoring my parents would just get me a *long* life, which I wasn't so sure I wanted. But there's a better *quality* of life that comes when we obey God by obeying and respecting our parents. We find a happiness we can't know otherwise. I wish I could explain how that works, but it's still a bit of a mystery to me. All I know is that God tells us the best way to play the game of life, and when we do it His way, we get to wear flowers in our hair. We get to enjoy a carefree love of life that comes when we've done all we can to spread peace in our families.

When we choose to honor our parents with our attitudes and actions, we make God proud. He, in turn, will bless us with a happier, more fulfilling life here on earth and even more extravagant rewards when we get to heaven. He doesn't promise to change our parents (bummer!), but He can and will change *our* hearts to be able to respond to our parents better, even when they are dead wrong. That's part of the secret, remember? Allowing every aspect of family life to make us more like Christ. As we discovered earlier in this chapter, God has put us in these flawed families so we can learn how to honor *Him*. So let's you and me leave our shoulder shrugging, eye rolling, door slamming, and name-calling in the past. I promise that your family relationships will be *much* better without them!

> *God, I admit that sometimes my attitude could use some adjusting. Sometimes my emotions just get the better of me. Fill my heart with Your love, patience, gentleness, and self-control so that when I don't agree with my parents, I won't react in a way that makes both You and me look bad. I want to learn how to submit to You through my parents' authority. And I want others—especially my family—to see You shine through me, in my attitude and actions. Help me love them the way I love You, God. Amen.*

Application Questions

1. *On a scale of 1 to 10, rate your attitude toward your parents, with 1 being "angelic" and 10 being "really rotten." Be honest!*

   1   2   3   4   5   6   7   8   9   10

2. *What circumstances and topics tend to spark a bad attitude in you?*

3. *When you're miffed at your parents over something, how do you express your—ahem—displeasure? (Feel free to check any and all that apply.)*

   ☐ *I accuse them of "not understanding."*

   ☐ *I use body language (slumping shoulders, stomping feet, and so on).*

   ☐ *I give the age-old eye roll.*

   ☐ *I tell them how they're wrong or being unfair.*

   ☐ *I rely on the infamous door slam. Works every time!*

   ☐ *I yell or argue.*

   ☐ *I go to my room and shut the door until I have to come out to eat.*

   ☐ *I threaten to run away, or I say I want to live with another parent or relative.*

   ☐ *Other:*

   ☐ *Other:*

4. *What do you think parents can do to make it easier for their kids to honor them?*

5. *You've already heard my suspicion about why God instructed kids to honor their parents before He gave any other rules for relationships. Do you agree? Explain why or why not.*

6. *What are your thoughts about the fifth commandment (honor your father and mother)? Do you think it's fair? Wise? Good for us? Are you're doing a good job of it?*

7. *The apostle Paul seems to use the words* obey *and* honor *interchangeably in Ephesians 6:13. What are the similarities between these two words? How are they different?*

8. *Write down a handful of things your parents have asked you to do this week (chores, schoolwork, babysitting, and so on). As you complete each task, cross it out. If you had a good attitude while you did it, draw a little smiley face next to the task. If you were a first-rate drama queen, put a little frowny face next to it.*

9. *Now list some intangible things your parents have asked of you, such as to have a good attitude, work hard, be nice to*

your brothers and sisters, and love God. Write down at least one practical way you can work at obeying each request.

10. *Have you ever watched a friend or sibling have a bad attitude toward his or her parents? How did it make that person look? This one may be a little tougher: How do you think the way you treat your parents makes you look?*

CHAPTER FIVE

Earning Trust (and Gaining Freedom)

INDEPENDENCE.

There's a whole lot o' punch in those twelve letters. It's a state of being, characteristic, and attitude all in one. And for a teenager, it also acts like a drug; it is addicting, gives us a rush, and makes us crave more and more of it to satisfy. That's not to say independence is a bad thing. No way! Independence is a good and natural part of growing up.

But here's the rub: Since the day you were born, you've been dependent on and subject to someone else. Think about it. You've always had an authority over you: a mom or dad who organized your social life, told you what you could and couldn't do, and monitored everything, from your food intake to your media output. Now that you're getting closer to being on your own, it makes sense that you feel an itch to push against that. You have your own opinions, style, and ideas about life, and you want to make your own decisions, whether good or bad. I get that. And so do your parents. (Probably. Most of the time?) The trouble comes when you and they disagree on just how much freedom you need and deserve as you get older. 'Cause in case you haven't noticed, we usually want more than our parents are willing to give.

If that describes you and your parents, this chapter is for you. I want to help you see what freedom really is and the responsibilities that come with it, as well as give you some tools to help you earn the trust you feel you deserve.

We may as well get the bad news out of the way: *Complete freedom?* No such thing.

I know that's painfully anticlimactic. But it's true—at least for us girls who want to live life God's way and get all the blessings that come with that lifestyle. Let me explain.

Complete Trust, Limited Freedom

I imagine that, at least for the most part, your parents trust you. But (wild guess here) do you think they have room to ease up on what they let you do, when they let you go, where they'll let you drive, and so on? If so, you're not alone. A lot of girls feel that way.

After years of talking to girls about family life, here's my observation: Just because you have your parents' trust does not mean they'll give you total freedom.

Hmmm . . . *limited freedom.*

That just sounds wrong, doesn't it? *Limited freedom* is an oxymoron—a statement that seems to contradict itself. Can a girl really be free if her parents put limits or boundaries on that freedom? Valid question.

To answer it, let's look at two other really important relationships in life. The first one is marriage.

I can honestly say that I trust my hubby, Paul, more than I trust any other person alive. Not only is he extremely good-looking (that doesn't have anything to do with trust—just a bonus fact), but he has also proven his character time and time again. When I got altitude sickness while backpacking on our honeymoon? He carried my pack *and his* the whole way down the mountain. He always asks me before making plans with the guys, just to make sure I'm cool with it. If I'm in a jam, he's the first one to my rescue. He tells me he loves me and that I'm beautiful E-V-E-R-Y day. When we buy a pint of our favorite ice cream, he leaves the last scoop for me (true love!). He's a man of integrity and justice, someone I can count on to do the right thing. Every. Single. Time. And he tells me he trusts me, too. Yet, despite our unfailing trust, we've set up some checks and balances in our relationship. We've *chosen* to give up some of our personal freedom to make sure we're on the up-and-up with each other. For example, we share passwords to all our e-mail and bank accounts. We ask each other's permission before we make big purchases so we don't make dumb decisions. We check in before making plans that would affect the other person.

Some might argue that our system shows we don't trust each other. I think the exact opposite is true. We love and trust each other *so* much that we can be mature enough to say, "I need accountability to make sure I'm doing what's right before God, and you're the perfect person for the job!" It's a *freeing* thing to trust someone so much that you can sacrifice some of your freedom to him or her for your own good.

A person's relationship with God is another surprising place where complete trust and limited freedom coexist. King David understood this paradox. Here's how he put it: "I will keep on obeying your instructions forever and ever. *I will walk in freedom*, for I have *devoted myself to your commandments*" (Psalm 119:44-45, emphasis added). Did you catch that? David found *freedom* by following God's teaching—teaching that actually kept David from doing whatever he wanted to do, whenever he wanted to do it.

When we choose to trust God completely and give our lives to Him, we have to give up some of our personal freedoms to obey His Word. If we're serious about giving our lives to God, we can't lie to get out of trouble or have sex with our boyfriends because we "really love them." But in giving up some of those freedoms, we are actually *freed*. Crazy, huh? Living God's way—trusting Him enough to let Him lead us—is the only way to experience the freedom of a clean conscience, bubbling joy, deep peace, and no regrets. In giving up some of those personal freedoms the world tells us will satisfy, we gain the greatest freedom of all.

Complete trust and limited freedom will exist in just about every important relationship you have in life.

Here's where it starts feeling unfair: In your relationship with your parents, limited freedom is *forced* on you, which— let's be honest—sometimes stinks up the place. God didn't pull you aside before you were born and ask, "So, daughter, which parents would you like to submit your freedom to? Go ahead and pick out the set you think will be the fairest." Wouldn't that have been nice? But as it is, God picked them out for you, and He tells you to trust Him in that choice. Never have the following verses been more true:

> Trust GOD from the bottom of your heart;
>   don't try to figure out everything on your own.
> Listen for GOD's voice in everything you do,
>   everywhere you go;
>   he's the one who will keep you on track.
> Don't assume that you know it all.

PROVERBS 3:5-7, MSG

To help put flesh on these verses, let's pretend for a minute that parents don't exist (try not to get too excited!). In this make-believe world where you get to create your own boundaries, would you stay true to what you know is right, or would you get yourself into trouble? Would you stay on top of everything or start slacking off? Check the boxes for the areas where you think you might need accountability:

- ☐ Boys
- ☐ Driving
- ☐ Getting homework done
- ☐ Phone/Internet use
- ☐ The people you hang out with
- ☐ The places where you hang out
- ☐ Eating well
- ☐ Other:

When I was in high school, I would have said I'd do just fine without my parents. I thought I was wise enough to make good decisions on my own, without my parents forcing them on me. But my decision-making track record tells a *slightly* different story. Here are just two (of many) examples.

The Dance

It was the summer before my freshman year of high school, and I was riding high. For the first time in my life, boys were actually starting to notice my existence—even one I thought was pretty cute. Okay, that's a huge understatement. He was stinkin' hot. And he happened to be the heartthrob of the little community I grew up in. All the girls—even the prettiest, most popular girls at school—had crushes on Dreamy Boy. At least that's how I remember it. He was tall, athletic, and two years older, and he had a smile that could melt an ice cube in a snowstorm. Positively dreamy. You can imagine my absolute hysteria when I heard that not only did Dreamy

Boy know I *existed*, but he might actually want to go out with me.

About this time, the local clubhouse announced a summer teen dance. I grew up in a really small town, so this was a big event for us kids. It's not like we had a movie theater or mall where we could hang out. I remember so clearly hearing from a friend that D.B. (for short) was hoping I'd be there. Hoping *I* would be there! My heart was all a-pitter-pattering. If I'd had any more butterflies in my stomach, I could have opened a conservatory. The minutes dragged on as I waited for the weekend to come. Then . . .

My dad said I couldn't go.

With one casual, unfair decision, Dad completely A-bombed my hope of popularity and romance. *How could he do this to me?* Oh, I tried every manipulation technique in the book: "But there are going to be chaperones there!" No luck. "I just want to go have a good time!" Also no luck. "But *whyyy?*" That one put Dad over the edge, and he gave me the one-more-word-and-you're-grounded-for-life look.

I spent the night of the dance in my room. In tears. Feeling disappointed and more than a little mad. As much as I had tried to convince my parents that I just wanted to "have some fun" at the dance, I knew that the real reason I wanted to go was because I was hoping to have a teen-movie-spectacular romantic moment on the dance floor with my crush. And since I couldn't be there, I was certain my love life was doomed forever.

I didn't know it then—neither did my parents—but they

saved me from what could have been a whole summer of regret. Looking back on it now, I realize that Dreamy Boy wasn't interested in me for who I was. He had quite the reputation as a ladies' man, and he wasn't a Christian. Sure, he was ultra-cute, but had I gone out with him, who knows how it would have changed the course of my life.

Not going to the dance hurt me that night, but going likely would have resulted in complete heartbreak later on.

I hate to admit it now—and I never would have admitted it then—but my parents were right not to let me go. They limited my freedom, and it ended up freeing me.

The Road Trip

Fast-forward five years. It was the end of my freshman year of college, and I was riding high once again. For the first time in my life, I had the freedom I craved. I could make my own decisions: go where I wanted to go and do what I wanted to do. I lived at school, made my own schedule, and my parents were now giving advice rather than setting rules.

Just before school was out for the summer, I met a handsome college student from San Diego—a smart, athletic rugby player with a killer smile and a red Mustang. Once again I was staring at "positively dreamy." You can imagine how my heart melted within my chest when he told me he liked me one night on a balcony overlooking the ocean and then kissed me. It was the teen-movie-spectacular romantic moment I had dreamed of. I knew deep down that I probably liked him for the wrong reasons, but he was so *cute*! And he treated me special. And no one was there to tell me no.

About this time, my parents needed to leave their car with a mechanic in San Diego. *Such luck*, I thought. While pretending it was a great sacrifice, I offered to take their car down and stay with this guy "friend" of mine while the car got fixed. The minutes dragged on as I waited for the weekend to arrive. Then . . .

Mom and Dad said I shouldn't go.

I actually considered what they said—for all of two seconds. In my newfound adult freedom, I decided I knew what was best for me and that spending a weekend with a guy I had only just met and knew all of *nothing* about would be good, innocent fun. *What could possibly go wrong?*

I hate to say it, but my parents were right. The weekend I couldn't wait for turned out to be a disaster, including awkward sleeping arrangements, a roommate fight (over my being there), more lies to my parents . . . oh, and I got lost and ended up unknowingly tanning at a nude beach. Did I mention the weekend was an epic fail? Looking back, I'm ashamed of my reckless decision. It went against every relationship boundary I had put up in my life—emotionally, physically, and spiritually—and I ended up with a broken heart as a souvenir. I'd *thought* I had good sense and impeccable judgment, but I obviously still didn't understand as a new adult that I needed to limit my freedom for my own good.

(Typing all this makes me want to crawl into a hole all

over again. Thank you for loving me despite my stupid life choices. Nothing but grace between you and me, right?)

God knows that as young women, we need protection from ourselves. No matter how mature we are, as teens we need guidance to help us establish and stay inside good boundaries. Even if we make good decisions 95 percent of the time, that other 5 percent can cause a lot of unnecessary heartache.

Protective Services

Your parents are responsible for protecting you from more than just yourself. Even if your parents trust *you* exclusively, sometimes they have to limit your freedom because of the outside dangers you face.

Can I show my vulnerability for a minute? (As if that last story *didn't*.)

I *really* didn't understand why my parents were "protective" until I became responsible for the safety of two beautiful, precious people myself. Becoming a parent changes how you see the world.

I know you're not totally in the dark about what goes on out there in this big, scary world. You hear the news. You know accidents happen. You understand there are evil people out there who would hurt you if they could. You know that the world isn't safe . . . *sort of.*

As teens, we have *ideas* about what's out there, but many of us also feel invincible. Many of us feel as if those are things that happen to *other* people. But when we become parents, we are faced with the sobering reality that *we* are responsible for protecting our kids from those unseen dangers. That's no easy job as our kids get more independent and leave the warm safety of a nest we've spent more than a decade building for them. (It's no excuse for helicopter parenting. Ultimately, every parent has to trust God with his or her kids' safety. But as kids, sometimes it helps to know that our parents have reasons for protecting us that we might not understand yet.)

Looking back, I was pretty naive to the dangers all around me. I'm glad that even though my parents trusted *me*, they didn't trust the people around me. The dance was one example. They didn't trust that the clientele of the local clubhouse would be the best influence on me, and they were absolutely right. In other situations, they protected me from drunk drivers, "friends" who weren't the best friends, an older guy who I *thought* just wanted to be friends, and probably a bunch of other compromising situations that I knew nothing about.

God gives us parents to help protect our hearts, bodies, and souls. If we buck against the protection God gives us through their rules, we only hurt ourselves. We need their protection, not because we're still five years old or weaklings, but because we're *human*. And as humans, we make mistakes. That's why we need limited freedom—imposed on us by our parents as we grow up and self-imposed as we get older.

Six Tips to Earn Trust

At this point, you may be thinking, *Yeah, that's all fine and good, Jessie, but I still think my parents should cut me a little more slack.* Fair enough. I realize some parents have a hard time trusting their daughters with even reasonable, age-appropriate freedom. Maybe they're having a hard time coming to terms with the fact that their little girl is growing up. Maybe an older child made some bad decisions, so they're more cautious this time around. Or maybe they remember how they abused *their* freedom and are afraid you'll do the same. Whatever their reasons, no girl wants to feel as though she isn't trusted by the very parents who are supposed to teach her how to grow up. So let me share six ways you can earn—and keep—your parents' trust.

Before you read this section, you might want to take a minute to fill out the "Can I Be Trusted?" quiz on pages 215–217. (If you're sharing this book, you can find a reproducible version at www.LifeLoveandGod.com/family).

Tip #1: Be Smart

This wins the award for the most obvious tip, but the best way to earn your parents' trust is to make wise choices. Prove that you can be trusted.

When you choose your friends carefully, keep up with your schoolwork, stay away from compromising situations, resist peer pressure, and don't let boys monopolize your thought life, your parents will be more willing to trust you. And that trust will—hopefully—translate into more freedom.

This usually takes much longer than we would like, but hang in there. Like learning to play an instrument or building a lifelong friendship, all things of great value are worth working toward and waiting for.

Tip #2: Be Open

This one might win the award for the *hardest* tip. If you want your parents' trust, you may have to give up some of that privacy you've been fighting for. I know that doesn't seem fair, or even decent, but track with me.

If Paul told me that he didn't want me to read his e-mails anymore, that he didn't feel I should have the password for his laptop, and that he wanted to go out with his guy friends but wouldn't tell me where, do you think I'd be a little suspicious? Um, *yeah*. More than a little, actually. Even though his requests wouldn't automatically mean he was doing anything shady, I would question my trust in him.

It's the same in your family. If you act secretive with your text messages, phone conversations, where you're going, and who you're going with, your parents are bound to wonder what you're up to, even if you're not doing anything wrong. But if you're open with those things, it shows you have nothing to hide.

Like I said, I know this is a difficult thing to ask of a teenager. You might feel as though you have no privacy left to give up! But embrace the paradox: The more privacy you're willing to sacrifice, the more privacy you'll actually gain in the long run as your parents learn to trust you and give you more freedom.

Tip #3: Be Considerate

considerate (kən-'si-də-rət) *adj.*—thoughtful of the rights and feelings of others[4]

As we learned in chapter 2, your parents are still people. They get worried, frustrated, and impatient, and they like it when others consider their feelings. If you want to earn your parents' trust, become a master at *politeness*. Give them a call when you're going to be late or when your plans change. Shoot them a text to ask if it's okay if you go to so-and-so's house, even though you're sure they'll say yes. This scores big—I mean *big*—points with the parental unit, because that's what adults do. Adults (should, at least) communicate when their actions are going to affect someone else. On the flip side, if an adult doesn't do those things, they are seen as self-centered and immature. For example, if an employee is going to be late for work and doesn't call to let her boss know, she'll soon be searching for a new job. Or if I don't let my friend know that we aren't going to make it to her house at the time we set, I might not get another invite.

So go out of your way to fill your parents in on your schedule and other details of your life. You don't have to give them minute-by-minute updates or divulge every single detail of your love life, but keep them up to speed on matters that concern them. You'll reap the rewards in trust points.

Tip #4: Tell the Truth

This should probably go without saying, but make sure that all the information you give your parents is *accurate*. Don't change the facts to make them happy, worry less, or say yes more often. Not only does God hate lying (see Proverbs 6:16-17), but bending the truth will undermine the trust you're trying to build with your parents. The truth always comes out eventually. Proverbs 12:19 says, "Truthful words stand the test of time, but lies are soon exposed."

That's a good reminder, isn't it? Our parents can learn to trust us only if we tell them the absolute truth, even when it might keep us from going where we want to go or doing what we want to do.

Tip #5: Be Respectful

Here's another really hard part of gaining your parents' trust. But as difficult as it is to execute this tip, if you don't get a handle on it, you'll have a slim-to-none chance of getting your parents to trust you. Are you ready?

Respect their decision when they tell you no.

When hearing my parents' unfavorable verdict, my first reaction was usually to moan, "But [insert favorite negotiation terms here]," sometimes accompanied by whining, foot stomping, eye rolling, or various accusations of how they never [fill in the blank]. At least in my experience, this tactic never actually works. From a parent's perspective, watching a daughter throw a tantrum because she wants more freedom kind of proves the point that she's too immature to handle more freedom. Right? Right.

I don't completely understand the magic here, but a simple "Okay"—nothing less, nothing more—works wonders in securing your parents' trust. If you respect their decision as parents, even if (*especially* if) you completely disagree with their reasoning, they'll be more likely to relent the next time around.

As I said, it's not easy. I'm just reporting the facts, because I want you to earn the trust and freedom you're going to need as you become an independent adult.

Tip #6: Be Patient

This tip is for those of you who find yourself in the unfortunate position of having to *re*-earn your parents' trust because you made one stupid choice (or many). (Been there!)

Unfortunately, losing your parents' trust defies mathematics. You would think that if you lost your parents' trust because of one bad decision, you should be able to earn it back by making one good decision. That would seem fair. And easier. But it takes about a hundred good decisions before a parent will forget that one bad one.

Regaining your parents' trust is daunting but doable. It's basically the same process as gaining their trust in the first place (i.e., the five tips we've talked about up to this point) but with one major factor added to the mix: *time*.

It's so hard to wait. Especially when you want them to trust you in time for the party you want to go to this weekend. Or before you turn thirty, for that matter.

If you haven't figured this out already, humans are not naturally patient creatures. We want what we want, and we want it right now. But re-earning trust is a lengthy process. So sit back, grab a good book, and commit to sticking with the plan no matter how long it takes. And while you're waiting, resist the temptation to sabotage your efforts with whining, pleading, begging, and a bad attitude to try to force their trust.

Live in Freedom

As impossible as it may seem now, one day you will have the freedom you want, either because your parents give it to you or because you'll be on your own. I hope that when that day comes you'll make Galatians 5:13 your life's anthem:

> You have been called to live in freedom, my brothers and sisters. But don't use your freedom to satisfy your sinful nature. Instead, use your freedom to serve one another in love.

According to this verse, every God follower should embrace limited freedom for the sake of love, just as Jesus did. Have you ever considered that during His time on earth, Jesus gave up His "divine privileges" and took the position of a slave? Why would a God who could do anything He wanted to humble himself like that? Philippians 2:6-8 gives us the answer:

> Though he was God,
>> he did not think of equality with God
>> as something to cling to.
> Instead, he gave up his divine privileges;
>> he took the humble position of a slave
>> and was born as a human being.
> When he appeared in human form,
>> he humbled himself in obedience to God
>> and died a criminal's death on a cross.

Jesus limited His freedom "in obedience to God." Put another way, Jesus limited His unlimitedness simply because God the Father wanted Him to. Can you wrap your mind around that kind of obedience?

As girls who want to grow to be more like Jesus, let's add "limited freedom" to our foundation. Let's be okay with putting aside our rights, wants, and privileges for the sake of obeying God.

As fun as it is to make your own decisions—and you'd best believe it's a whole barrel of fun!—for the sake of holiness and the good of others, I hope you'll choose to limit your ability to do, be, love, and buy what you want to. 'Cause that's where *true* freedom is found.

Hi, God. You know I feel ready for more freedom in my life. Help me show my parents I can be trusted and

*then keep their trust. I also know that I'm not perfect
or invincible and that I need my parents' rules and
protection sometimes. I want to be the kind of girl who
makes wise choices and is okay with limited freedom
for my own good. Show me how to use the freedom I do
have to love others well and bring You glory. Amen.*

Application Questions

1. *Have you ever considered that once you live on your own, you
   still might not have complete freedom? Can you think of some
   examples where you'll have limited freedom as an adult?*

2. *Have you given up some of your personal freedoms in order
   to follow God's laws? What have you given up? How has
   giving up those things actually brought you more freedom?*

3. *Have you or someone you know ever taken freedom too far
   and paid a price for it in the end?*

4. Have your parents ever told you that you couldn't go some-
    where that you really wanted to go and, in the end, their
    decision kept you from getting hurt?

5. What people, places, and things are your parents responsible
    to protect you from?

6. In your professional teenage opinion, is it better to have
    parents who are protective, lenient, or somewhere in the
    middle? Why? How would you describe your parents?

7. *If you feel your parents have a hard time trusting you, can you see any reasons they might feel that way?*

8. *Are you in a position where you have to earn back your parents' trust? Based on everything we've talked about in this chapter, write in your journal a game plan for re-earning their trust.*

9. *Can you think of anyone you know who gained independence and then lived however he or she wanted, regardless of the consequences? What can you learn from that person's choices?*

CHAPTER SIX

Becoming the Best Big Sister

UP TILL NOW, we've been talking a lot about your parents: how to understand them, respect them, and get them to trust you. But there are probably other individuals in your home who may or may not occasionally make you want to jump off a cliff.

If you have brothers or sisters—whether blood, step-, half, adopted, or foster—you know that the dynamics between siblings have the potential to create a whole lot of crazy around the house.

In this chapter, I'm going to lay out some things you can do to be a good big sister; in chapter 7, we'll turn the tables and talk about what it takes to be a remarkable little sis. If you're an only child, I still recommend listening in. You never know what "siblings" God will bring into your life down the road—whether through blood, adoption, or the big, beautiful family of God.

Before we get to some tips, I can't resist telling a little story that does a fair job of capturing the not-so-sweet essence of siblinghood.

Maybe you know about the family pecking order brothers and sisters tend to create. The oldest is usually at the top of the hierarchy and gets gobs of delight from lording it over, talking down to, and picking on the next oldest. Every time a sibling joins the family, he or she files in at the bottom and the one who used to be at the bottom sighs in relief before turning his or her sights on the new prey.

My three older stepbrothers had their hierarchy all figured out: Erin was at the top and picked on Ian, who was two years younger. Then Henry was born, and Ian was able to pass on his title of most vulnerable to the new youngest, paying forward all the torture. When my mom and stepdad got married and I became the new youngest, Henry assumed that his five-year-old stepsister was the new scapegoat. Never mind that I was a girl and, having been an only child, wasn't used to teasing and roughhousing. After seven years of being the youngest, Henry had no pity on me. He did everything he could think of to get under my skin. He was a master of pushing my buttons and would bring me to tears by threatening to cut off the head of my favorite stuffed animal or shoot my Barbies with a BB gun.

I was completely innocent, of course. (At least that's how I remember it. My brothers have since told me that I was inclined to be a brat and told Mom about Every. Thing. They. Did. I've also since come to appreciate them as pretty spectacular brothers. But *that doesn't play into this story.*)

Because I was a—ahem—*slight* tattletale, they learned to play certain "games" (aka torture) with me where I couldn't scream for help to get them in trouble. My absolute least favorite was when Erin would pin me down, flat on my back (which wasn't hard to do, as he was six years older), and then stick his smelly foot just an inch or so above my face. The other two boys would laugh and laugh as Erin would chide, "Kiss Mr. Big Toe!"

I was really in a pickle.

Under no circumstances did I want to touch my lips to that big, nasty toe. But if I opened up my mouth (even slightly) to scream for help, I knew he would stick that sucker right in.

Sometimes I still have nightmares about the feel of a calloused big toe against my trembling lips.

Boys. I tell ya.

You can imagine my excitement when my younger sister was born. She was the cutest little blonde you ever saw, with big brown eyes and freckles that melted Daddy's heart. She was also *the new youngest*, and it was finally my turn to pay it forward.

To my credit, I wasn't nearly as cruel to Alicia as the boys had been to me (she and I were, after all, young *ladies*), but I did recycle a few tricks of the trade for the sake of tradition.

One such family heirloom passed down to my little sis was—
you guessed it—Mr. Big Toe.

But the first time I tried this trick on my sister, the joke
was on me. For some reason I thought keeping my shoe on
might be less cruel than a bare toe (for her and for me). So
I pinned her down and dangled a shoed foot over her face. I
got ready to see her squirm and cower under my power as I
chided, "Kiss Mr. Big Toe!" But she didn't fight me. She just
puckered up and kissed the rubber.

Completely anticlimactic!

Didn't she realize that I had waited years to feel some measure of control over someone younger than I was? Nope. She
thought it was fun because her big sister was playing a game
with her. (I must have starved that poor girl of attention!) She
looked up to me so much that she was willing to kiss my shoe
on command. Oh, the power older siblings hold.

The game with Alicia went on for some time like that.
Some days she'd fight it, but other times she'd outwit me and
comply. That squirrelly little girl had more feistiness than I'd
anticipated, though, and one day she not only put her lips
to my shoe, she bit right through my favorite pair of sneak-
ers! I couldn't believe it. Her teeth—right through my white
canvas tennis shoes.

And that was the end of Mr. Big Toe. In one act of wit
and courage, my little sister put an end to the cycle of torture.

Sometimes, it takes only one.

I know it might sound impossible now, but pecking
orders, torture, teasing, and tormenting don't have to be

a major part of sibling life. You can, in fact, have healthy relationships with your brothers and sisters, and sometimes all it takes is for one of you to start the change. True, you don't have control over how your brothers and sisters act, speak, or treat you or each other. But don't underestimate the power of one girl who loves God, treats others with respect, and refuses to get tired of doing good (see Galatians 6:9). And when you're an older sister, your potential to change the atmosphere at your house gets supersized, because you're already in a position of influence.

Your Family's Top Model

If you're like me, when you think of the word *model,* you might picture paper-thin ladies strutting down a catwalk in eccentric fabrics that would never pass for clothes in the real world. Or maybe your mind turns to busty, lingerie-clad women pasted larger than life on storefront windows. Those are models, in one sense of the word. But if you're a big sister, did you know that you also carry the title?

> **model** ('mädl) *noun*—an example for imitation or emulation[5]

If you have little brothers or sisters, they're watching your life to see what they can copy, match, or do better than. Just as a model walks down the runway to show us examples of the latest fashions, you as an older sister are in the limelight, setting an example of the "hottest trends" in attitude and actions. The eyes of your younger brothers and sisters are glued to you, whether you like it or not.

Here's the scary part: In a fashion show, a model has to endure walking in stilettos down the catwalk for only a few minutes; her all-the-rage outfit will be forgotten by the time the next fashion expo rolls around. But in the world of family, you're in the spotlight every minute of every day. Younger siblings pick up on *everything* you do, say, and believe. They're aware of the way you view your body and how you feel about your relationship status. They notice how you talk to your parents and whether you read your Bible. They can name the types of friends you hang out with and the music you listen to. Even on those days when you know you're failing big-time, they're still watching.

Being a big sister is a big responsibility!

I don't know about you, but for a lot of my years at home, I didn't really take that responsibility seriously. It took me a long time before I looked outside my own little world to see just what an influence I had on my younger sister. For too long, she looked up to me and I (sort of) tolerated her existence. I know—great big sister. It breaks my heart now to think of the years I wasted by not investing in her the way I could have! Thankfully, I did get over myself eventually, when I discovered a passage of Scripture that has helped guide all the years since:

> Be an example to all believers in what you say, in
> the way you live, in your love, your faith, and your

purity. . . . Focus on reading the Scriptures . . . ,
encouraging the believers, and teaching them.

1 TIMOTHY 4:12-13

The apostle Paul wrote those words to his spiritual "little
brother," Timothy. Paul encouraged him to be the absolute
best example he could be for other Christians to follow. I
can't think of any better advice for you and me as we figure
out how to be good examples for our younger siblings too.
So let's personalize those eight directives, shall we?

#1: Be an Example in What You Say

The words that come out of your mouth have the power
to heal or to destroy. The third chapter of James talks a ton
about getting control of our tongues, because small words
can cause great damage. That's especially true with our little
siblings! Here's what James said:

> A word out of your mouth may seem of no account,
> but it can accomplish nearly anything—or destroy
> it! It only takes a spark, remember, to set off a forest
> fire. A careless or wrongly placed word out of your
> mouth can do that.   JAMES 3:5-6, MSG

How do you talk when your little brothers and sisters are
around? What kinds of subjects do you talk about? What stories do you tell? Are you careful with what you say *about* them?
How about your tone of voice? If you're not sure whether you're
setting a great example in what you say (and how you say it),
here are a few more questions to get you thinking:

- [ ] *Would it seem weird if you heard your little brother or sister saying the same words and phrases you say?*
- [ ] *Do your parents ever have to correct you for stuff you say around your siblings?*
- [ ] *Matthew 15:18 says, "The words you speak come from the heart." What do your words and your most frequent topics of conversation say about what's going on inside your heart?*

Now let's look at the second half of the verse: "A word out of your mouth may seem of no account, but *it can accomplish nearly anything*" (James 3:5, MSG, emphasis added). Your words also have the power to do some serious good, so—even though I know I'm going out of order (apologizing to you, OCD friends)—let's look at encouragement next.

#2: Be an Example in Encouragement

Last week a friend of mine gave me a little letter just because. In 151 words, she took me from feeling frazzled and lame as a wife, mother, writer, and human being (it had been one of those weeks!) to feeling supported, confident, talented, and loved. Tears welled up in my eyes as she pointed out the very things I felt I had bombed and instead showed me how I inspired her in each one. She wrapped up the note with "I want to remind you that you, too, are special and loved." Holy blown away! I just read it right now and got teary yet again.

That's the power of words!

"So encourage each other and build each other up" (1 Thessalonians 5:11). Why not? Tell your little brother he's really good at building Lego towers or drawing dinosaurs. Write your sister a note just to tell her you love her and that she's beautiful.

I *still* remember a compliment my brother Ian gave me when I was a teenager. He said, "Very few girls can pull off being a tomboy—athletic and out there doing stuff—and still be feminine and beautiful." To me, that was the best compliment ever, and it changed how I viewed myself. His words made me walk a little taller. So make an effort to point out the good and gently, *humbly*, caution against the bad. Use your words to make your siblings more confident in themselves, hopeful for the future, and sure of your love for them. Because they likely look up to you, you have an unequaled power to encourage them to be their best, try their hardest, and understand how precious they are.

#3: Be an Example in the Way You Live

We've all heard the saying "Actions speak louder than words." That's definitely true in our relationships with our brothers and sisters! Just like faith without actions is dead (see James 2:14, 17), telling our siblings about truth while living opposite of it won't do a pinch of good.

For example, you can tell your little brother that smoking, drinking, or ditching school is a bad idea, but it will look like a good one if he sees you doing it. You can tell your little sister she's being silly for having a crush on her fifth-grade substitute teacher, but if you talk about guys all the time, she'll think being boy crazy is normal.

How about some less obvious actions that can be just as influential? Have you thought about the way you can model a work ethic, treat your parents with respect, or keep a lid on strong emotions? Can you think of any other areas where you can be a good example?

#4: Be an Example in Love

The Greek word for love that Paul used in 1 Timothy 4:12, *agape*, describes a love shown through affection (a caring tenderness) and benevolence (acts of kindness).[6] So we're not talking about romantic love here but rather the kind of caring and kindness a girl should have for the people around her, including her brothers and sisters.

Did you know that people feel most loved in different ways? Author Gary Chapman coined the term *love languages* to describe the ways people feel loved.[7] He says that some people feel most cared for when someone gives them a gift. Others feel most loved by spending quality time with someone or when a person does an act of service for them. Physical touch and affirming words are two other common ways people feel loved. The trick for us, then, is to figure out the way the people around us feel loved so we can show them love in the best way. If you're not sure how your siblings feel most loved, try this spattering of ideas and see which ones seem to have the most bearing. Even if you're not hitting the bull's-eye of their love language, any of these will have a positive effect!

Spend time together:

- Watch a movie (let him pick which one).
- Invite her to spend time in your room, or hang out in hers.
- Read him a book or take a bike ride together.
- Tell her about what's going on in your life—what you're excited about or struggling with. Then ask her some meaningful questions.

Speak love:

- Each day this week, tell him one reason you admire and respect him.
- Make an acrostic of her name, giving one thing you love about her for each letter.
- Tell him "I love you" just because.
- Write her a little note of encouragement.

Serve:

- Offer to do his chores today.
- Take her plates to the kitchen after dinner.
- Help him with his homework.
- Teach her skills that you know how to do (e.g., some dance moves or your free-throw technique).

Sacrifice:

- Give up your turn to ride shotgun.
- Let her borrow your favorite _____ (dress, book, curling iron, and so on).

- Take a few extra minutes in your devotions to pray for him.
- Buy something for her instead of for yourself.

#5: Be an Example in Faith

As a big sister, you have a huge opportunity to be a light for Jesus to your younger brothers and sisters. Maybe they know that you call yourself a Christian, but do you talk about God around them? Do you pray for them (privately or together)? Do they see you making decisions based on what you think God would want?

The words you say and the way you live have the potential to make an *eternal* impression on your younger siblings. So set a good example of faith! Show them that following God with their lives is the best decision they can ever make.

#6: Be an Example in Purity

If you live in the twenty-first century and have spent much time at a church, the word *purity* probably brings to mind promise rings and youth-group talks about saving sex for marriage. And although keeping sex in its proper place is a part of purity here in 1 Timothy 4:12, the Greek word Paul uses, *hagneia*, does even *more* heart housecleaning. Hagneia doesn't mean only sexual purity; it includes being free from anything that doesn't belong in your heart, such as greed, selfishness, laziness, lying, jealousy, and worshiping anything or anyone other than God. Can you say "high standard"? Yeah, that list intimidates me, too!

The truth is, we're not going to get it right 100 percent of the time. We're still growing and learning to let go of sin in our hearts. But even though we're not perfect, we can *still* be good examples to our little brothers and sisters by owning up to our mistakes and showing them what it looks like to get serious about ditching our sin.

So let me ask you this: When you think about the influences in your life—music, media, friends, guys—is there anything you surround yourself with that is keeping you from having a completely pure heart? Next question: Are you willing to give up those things to better your relationship with God? If your answer is yes, I have good news! Not only will you set a great example for your little siblings to follow, but you'll also benefit from one of God's big promises: "God blesses those whose hearts are pure, for they will see God" (Matthew 5:8).

#7: Be an Example in Reading the Bible

Consistently reading the Bible is challenging—that's no secret!—and unfortunately I don't have any shortcuts for you. To dig in and soak up the truth, a girl has to have discipline and motivation. But the rewards are *so* worth it! As you learn and grow through reading God's Word, your life will be transformed. And as your life is transformed, your family will notice. Your example of faithfulness to God's Word will make an impact, even if you don't see it right away.

#8: Be an Example in Teaching

We older sisters are notorious for being bossy. We easily catch what I call Mean Mom Syndrome: feeling as if it's

If you're not sure where to start reading your Bible, I have some ideas for you. Head on over to www.LifeLoveandGod.com and search "Bible reading."

our duty to watch our little brothers and sisters like hawks, quickly pointing out what they're doing wrong and then nagging them until they change. It's actually pretty freeing to let go of that mentality and stick to being a sister instead of a parent. (I know you might not have the luxury of having good parents to look out for your little brothers and sisters, and my heart goes out to you if you really *do* have to be "Mom" in your house. But you can ditch the "mean" part.)

So how can we be examples in teaching if we're not in charge? We can wait to be asked! If we resist the urge to boss everyone around, others might come to us for advice when they need it. Now, if we dole out advice based on our own puny human knowledge, we're not going to be much help. Instead, we should know the Bible so well that we can offer others *God's* wisdom when they need advice. *That's* being an example in wise teaching.

Check out these words Paul wrote to Timothy in another letter:

> All Scripture is inspired by God and is useful to
> teach us what is true and to make us realize what is

wrong in our lives. It corrects us when we are wrong and teaches us to do what is right. God uses it to prepare and equip his people to do every good work.

2 TIMOTHY 3:16-17

God's Word teaches us everything we need to know about how to live lives that honor Him, bless others, and make us happiest. You ready to practice this? Think about an issue that a younger brother or sister is facing. Is he being bullied at school? Does she like a guy she shouldn't? What advice can you give him or her, based on what you know is true from the Bible?

The Power of Influence

The times I spent with my brothers weren't all torture (thank you, Jesus!). In fact, as the years went on (read: we all grew up a little), Erin's big toe stopped making appearances, Ian became a confidant, and Henry taught me to embrace life and live a little dangerously (in a good way).

What's amazing to me is how little effort it takes for big brothers and sisters to make a lifelong impact on their siblings. Ian was a perfect example of this. When I was a teenager, he'd sometimes take me on "dates" to show me how a guy should treat me. Sweet, right? Over dinner or miniature golf, he asked me questions, opened doors for me, and always paid for everything. When he enlisted in the Marines, he'd write me letters telling me about his life and encouraging me in mine. He'd give advice about everything from boyfriend stuff to dealing with drama at home. I *loved* it. And I loved *him* for it.

Ian used his influence as my big brother to build my confidence, show me love, and teach me the ropes of life. I was thankful then, and I am thankful now. He still calls me often just to say hello and see how I'm doing.

No matter how crummy your past has been with your siblings, it's never too late to start being a good big sister. All it takes is a little forethought, a dash of selflessness, and a big dose of love. You might be surprised at how much good you can do in their lives!

I realize that you may still be thinking, *But Jessie, you don't know* my *little brother (or sister). He (or she) is really, really [circle adjective of your choice: annoying, gross, bossy, moody, weird, rude, mean, other: _____].* And you may in fact have a harder-to-deal-with-than-most situation. But I've said it before, and I'm sure I'll say it again: When it comes to the difficult things in life, God doesn't excuse us from living His way. If we'll let Him, He'll use those difficult situations to make us more like His Son, Jesus, who is *our* example— our model. And that's what all this family stuff is about, remember? The whole point of being a big sister is (just like everything else) to allow God to do His work in us *through* our families. (Yes, even when they're super-annoying.) So rather than fight it, let's embrace the responsibilities and joys of big sisterhood.

*Dear Father, thank You for choosing to make me part
of Your family and giving me the best Big Brother ever!
I want to learn from Jesus' example so that I can be
a better example to my little siblings in every area of
my life. Keep working on my heart, God, making me
more patient, understanding, and loving for Your glory.
Amen.*

Application Questions

1. *What funny memories do you have of your younger siblings
   making their mark on your life?*

2. *Do your younger brothers and sisters look up to you? How
   can you tell?*

3. *How would you rate the example you've been setting lately for your younger siblings, with 1 being "terrible example" and 10 being "top model"?*

   1   2   3   4   5   6   7   8   9   10

4. *If your younger siblings were going to fill out a report card for your performance as a big sis, how would you score? For each category, give yourself a letter score based on how you think you're doing. Then write down two practical action points you can put into practice this week that would improve your grade.*

Category	Grade	Action Points
Example: **Words**	*B-*	• *Tell Mackenzie that she did a really good job at her soccer game.*
Words		
Encouragement		
Actions		
Love		
Faith		
Purity		
Bible Reading		
Teaching		

5. *In your journal, take some time to talk with God about your relationships with your younger siblings. Be honest about how you're feeling and ask Him to change your heart if it needs to be changed. Be sensitive to what He might ask of you in return: maybe to apologize to your little brother for something you've said or spend an afternoon with your little sister. You can write as much or as little as you need to, but don't rush.*

CHAPTER SEVEN

Becoming the Best Little Sister

WHEN I WAS in elementary school, no matter how terribly my three older brothers teased and tortured me, I still wanted to be one of the gang. Part of their inner circle, you know? I wanted to be "in" on their inside jokes, to be the fourth musketeer. It's not like they had any grand adventures or FBI missions or anything, but the games they played always seemed so much more fun than My Little Pony because they were the *big kids*. Everything they did fascinated me. On any given Saturday, I'd be quite content to play by myself until I saw them doing something together. Then whatever I was doing seemed like baby stuff. Child's play. *Bor-ing*.

Of course, my big brothers didn't want their little sister to butt in and ruin the fun, which made me all the more desperate to get in the club. That was my first mistake. Big brothers (and sisters, too) can sniff out desperation a mile away, and they'll use your eagerness against you, yessiree. Because my big brothers knew I'd do anything to be able to play with them, they could get me to do things I'd never otherwise do.

One time my big brothers formed a secret club. *A secret club!* How is a little sister supposed to hear that and still be content to play with her dolls? Naturally I just *had* to be in it. I begged and pleaded until they were finally open to negotiations. "Okay, fine," they conceded. "You can be in the club . . . *if* you drink the secret potion." I was elated. All I had to do was drink something and I'd be in on the fun. It all seemed too easy—until I watched them concoct the secret potion.

The three boys raided the fridge, pouring any liquids they could find into a plastic cup. Milk, pickle juice, ketchup, jelly—*yuuuuum*. They put the finishing touches on their brew, and we headed to the secret hideout (aka under the staircase of our apartment complex) for the inauguration. As excited as I was to finally be a member of their secret club, the price of admission was steep. Just the smell of that foul mixture made me want to hurl. I stood completely still, plastic cup in hand, for what seemed like ten years.

"Come on, just do it!" my brothers urged.

I rallied all the courage a six-year-old can muster and touched the rim of the cup to my lips. *Do I really want to do this?* My better sense tried to warn me. But I heard the boys' voices over my thumping heart: "Come on, Jess, we don't have all day!" A surge of adrenaline, a deep breath, and I sent the secret potion tumbling down my throat.

It was as nasty as I'd imagined it would be, but it was also my proudest moment. Not only did I drink it, I didn't puke it up. There were high fives all around for my accomplishment.

It didn't take long, though, to realize that being a member of my brothers' secret club didn't change much. My bravery didn't erase that part where they didn't want their pesky little sis to play with them. The whole ordeal was just a trick to get me to drink the nastiest cocktail they could create.

Ah, well. You live and you learn, right?

I did learn, and as I grew up, I grew out of secret-club-crashing and other desperate attempts to be one of the boys. But that desire to be accepted—to feel equal, to know that I belonged—never went away. As a teen, I still wanted them to like me. I wanted them to think I was cool and fun to be with and good at sports like they were. So I tried to act like I wasn't nervous and insecure when I was around them and their friends at football games. I pretended not to care that people were drinking at parties we went to. I'd shoot hoops with them and my dad, even though somehow I *always* got hit in the face with the basketball before the game was over. (Seriously. E-V-E-R-Y time. Square in the nose. It has become a long-standing family joke.)

If you have older brothers or sisters, I bet you have your own list of things you've done to impress them or get them to notice and accept you.

In chapter 6, I shared how to be a stellar big sister by

setting a good example. But I realize that your older sibs may not have that figured out yet. In fact, most of them probably have no clue just how much influence they hold over their younger siblings and aren't living their lives as "an example to all believers" (1 Timothy 4:12). So if you have one or more kids above you on the family totem pole, let's talk about how you can take full advantage of your role as a younger sister, whether your older sibs are the best in the world or not-so-great examples to follow.

Copy the Good, Learn from the Bad

Midway through our honeymoon, Paul and I found ourselves driving across the fine state of Nevada. (Our honeymoon was an epic five weeks of sand, snow, airplanes, and a teal-green Honda Civic, spanning 3,500 miles and a half dozen campgrounds while we waited for our jobs to start.) Being rather outdoorsy, we thought it would be fun to take a "quick" hike in the Ruby Mountains to Liberty Pass, so we took a detour to the trailhead and laced up our tennis shoes. We weren't really dressed for hiking up a mountain pass, but such things don't stop you when you're young and in love. Neither do snowfields, apparently, which happened to be blocking whole sections of the trail because it was late spring. No, we were determined to make it to the top, trail or no trail. It was only three miles, after all.

A few *hours* later, we were still picking our way through downed trees, around the Dollar Lakes, and across snowy sections that covered the trail (at least we *hoped* the trail was under there somewhere!). Paul was about fifteen feet in front of me, crossing a long section of snow. I was bringing up the rear and happily admiring his, um, rear as he led the way toward the 12,400-foot notch we were aiming for. So he was walking along—step, step, step—and then—*whoosh!*—his next step broke through a layer of ice over a deep snowdrift and he dropped up to his armpits in snow. I don't remember if I screamed. It's possible. But I do remember laughing hysterically, Paul's head and outstretched arms the only things visible in a fifty-square-foot field of white snow. Of course, having a great sense of humor, he made me take a picture before pulling him out. I'll tell you one thing, though: I'm glad it wasn't me!

Sometimes there are benefits to following.

In fact, one of the best parts of being a little sister is that you have someone ahead of you on the trail of life. You get to watch your big brothers and sisters make decisions, so you see what works and what doesn't. You can be a student, studying how their decisions play out but skipping the consequences when they turn out to be dumb moves.

The apostle John encouraged his readers to keep their eyes open and take note of the examples of others, good and bad. He said,

> Dear friend, don't let this bad example influence you. Follow only what is good. Remember that those who do good prove that they are God's children, and those who do evil prove that they do not know God.   3 JOHN 1:11

Don't let bad examples influence you. Follow good examples. What a perfect verse for little sisters to take to heart!

So if your older brother starts hanging out with friends who smoke, drink, and talk about dirty stuff, watch and learn. How does that decision affect your brother? Your family? Or if your sister spends every waking hour on her phone, texting, listening to music, and dealing with friend drama, watch and learn. What is she missing out on? What could you do differently?

On the flip side, if your brother studies hard and says no to hanging out with friends on the weekends so he can get good grades at college, watch how it plays out. Is it worth the sacrifice? Or if your sister decides to end a relationship because her boyfriend is pressuring her to do stuff or has a hot temper, be a student. Is that an example you should follow?

I hope your older brothers and sisters are leading the way and showing you the *best* way to live your life. But even if they're not, be smart. You are in charge of your life choices and are the one who has to live with the results. So make decisions that are best for you.

Comparison: Alicia's Story

Being a little sister has another unique challenge: comparison. Sometimes it can be really hard not to compare yourself with an older brother or sister. Other times you might feel as if other people do the comparing for you. Other people, meaning your parents, teachers, coaches, aunts, uncles, youth pastors, grandparents, neighbors, bosses, complete strangers—did I leave anyone out? In an age when you're trying to earn your independence and be your own person, to feel like you're constantly in the shadow of an older sibling can be extremely discouraging and frustrating. I get that.

My brothers lived primarily with their mom, which meant I didn't go to school with them, which meant I didn't have to walk the halls of my high school dodging their shadows. My little sister, on the other hand, had to endure the painful experience of going to the same high school her big sister had gone to a few years before. More than any of us, she really felt the brunt of comparison in our family, so I've asked her to share a bit about her experience. Please welcome my amazing little sister, of mad makeup skills and biting-shoe fame, Alicia Jewett!

The Comparison Game

By Alicia Jewett

When you grow up with an older sibling who has measured up to all (or almost all) of your parents' standards (such as my sister), you feel as if you are being compared to something that is unattainable yet expected of you. You hear your parents say that no two kids are alike and that they have to learn how to raise each one individually, but it seems that they forget that when it comes to things like, say, sports. Or grades, interests, boyfriends, jobs, standards—basically just life in general.

At school I felt a constant comparison. In my case, it

wasn't so much a feeling as it was actually hearing, "Jess was the best volleyball player ever; why aren't you?" "Jess always got perfect grades; why can't you?" "Jess walked on water; why don't you?" You get the picture. Maybe in the back of my mind, I was afraid that I wasn't going to be as good as she was, so I decided to do the exact opposite of whatever she had done. I even stopped trying to do things really well, because if I failed, it wouldn't be as much of a letdown and I would have something to blame my failure on. I still find myself struggling with that; it really becomes a habit.

When you feel as though your parents are constantly comparing you to an older, godlike sibling, you naturally start making the comparisons yourself. It affects your self-esteem because you tend to start thinking that because they obviously want you to be like your sibling, they must like that child better. (Not that I'm trying to blame them. Although it sure would be nice to have something to blame all those insecure moments on!) You start to think that you can't be all that great if they're trying to change you. The way you are is not good enough. In my own case, I took it out on myself, and because I wasn't a Christian for most of this time, I turned to things like cutting. I even attempted suicide. I also gravitated toward people who didn't know my older sister so they wouldn't compare me to her and chose "second moms" who would treat me like *me*.

Being different can be a good thing. The danger for me, though, was that because my older sister was so "good" (at least she seemed to be to the rest of us) and was going down "the right path," I began to go down the wrong path because I was determined to be exactly the opposite of her. I compromised a lot of my initial personality just to make sure I was different from her.

Even though I complained a lot about having an older sister whom others expected me to live up to, secretly I wanted to be just like her. (I still do, most of the time.) Out of everyone in the family, she was who I looked up to the most, and I would do things that I knew would make her proud. Ultimately, I really wanted her approval above anyone else's and was, without a doubt, proud to be her sister.

Man, I love that girl—and not just because she made me tear me up with that last paragraph. My sister has a way of keeping it real, and she makes me laugh about my own shortcomings like nobody else can.

Can you relate to Alicia's story? Do you ever feel that you're expected to live up to an impossible standard set by an older brother or sister? Or maybe your older sib made some bad choices and you feel as though your parents are comparing you to him or her, expecting you to make the same mistakes?

From athletics to academics, attitude to aptitude, the adults in your life are likely to make at least a few comparisons between you and your older siblings. It's just one of those facts of life that you can't escape completely. Is it fair? No. But you can still live a full and satisfying life, even if your older brother *is* a genius or your sister can dance circles around you. No matter what comparisons others make, don't fall into the trap of feeling that you don't measure up. Instead, live out this verse:

We will not compare ourselves with each other as if one of us were better and another worse. We have far more interesting things to do with our lives. Each of us is an original.   GALATIANS 5:26, MSG

I love this verse! You and I have far more exciting and interesting things to do with our lives than constantly compare ourselves to our family members (or anyone else, for that matter).

You're an original.

So be you.

I know you're still figuring out who you are. We all are! That's why I'm including The "Me" Quiz II in the following pages: to help you think about who you are and who you want to be, apart from your older siblings. (You'll find the original "Me" Quiz in the first LIFE, LOVE & GOD book, *Crushed: Why Guys Don't Have to Make or Break You.*)

A few thoughts before you begin. This quiz is designed to get you thinking about who you really are. There are no right or wrong answers. You can be as straightforward or flowery as you need, and you can interpret each question however you'd like. I only suggest that you be completely honest, since no one else will ever read this. In other words, be you! This is for you and for God.

I've given you space to record your answers here, but if you plan to lend this book to a friend, feel free to write your answers in your journal instead.

Have fun!

THE "ME" QUIZ II

My full name is: _____

If I couldn't _____ ,
I just might die.

When someone says something that hurts me, I usually:
_____
_____

I think _____ is a good role model
*because:*_____
_____
_____

Sometimes I wish I didn't have to: _____
_____
_____

The top five characteristics I hope people see in me are:

1. _____
2. _____
3. _____
4. _____
5. _____

People would probably describe me as:

1. _____
2. _____
3. _____

If I had a whole day to do whatever I wanted with whomever I wanted, I'd: _____

_____

_____

My idea of a perfect vacation would be: _____

_____

_____

_____

My five favorite things to do are:

1. _____
2. _____
3. _____
4. _____
5. _____

My favorite kind of music is: _____

_____

My favorite things to read are: _____

_____

My favorite things to watch are: _____

_____

If you ran into me on a Saturday, I'd probably be wearing:

_____

_____

You couldn't pay me enough money to: _____

_____

_____

But I would *pay* money to: _____

_____

_____

If I had a private jet, the first place I'd fly would be: _____

_____

_____

The hardest thing about my family is: _____

_____

_____

If I could ask each of my siblings one question, I'd ask:

_____

_____

I'm thankful my mom is: _____

_____

_____

I'm thankful my dad is: _____

_____

_____

FAMILY

I think my parents could do this differently:_____

_____

_____

_____

If I have a family someday, I hope I'll: _____

_____

_____

_____

_____

These are the top five qualities I'd want in a future husband:

1. _____
2. _____
3. _____
4. _____
5. _____

In five years, I hope I: _____

_____

_____

_____

_____

The top five things I'd like to do someday are:

1. _____
2. _____
3. _____
4. _____
5. _____

In ten years I hope I:_____

_____

_____

_____

If I had ten million dollars, I would:_____

_____

_____

If I could learn one new sport or skill, it would be: _____

_____

If I could be friends with only three people, I'd choose:

    1. _____

    2. _____

    3. _____

The best compliment someone has ever given me is: _____

_____

I wish more people would: _____

_____

_____

I feel really bad for people who:_____

_____

_____

When it comes to school, my philosophy is:_____

_____

_____

Going to school without makeup on would:_____
_____
_____

When I think about God, I'm most grateful for: _____
_____
_____
_____

I think God made me because:_____
_____
_____
_____

I think ultimate happiness comes from: _____
_____
_____
_____

By the time I finish reading this book, I hope: _____
_____
_____
_____

I think this quiz was:_____
_____
_____
_____

At times you may feel like your only identity is being known as _____'s little sister, but as you focus on your unique strengths, characteristics, beauty, and accomplishments, you can be proud of who you are and who you're becoming.

Let these words be a challenge:

> Make a careful exploration of who you are and the
> work you have been given, and then sink yourself
> into that. Don't be impressed with yourself. Don't
> compare yourself with others. Each of you must take
> responsibility for doing the creative best you can
> with your own life.   GALATIANS 6:4-5, MSG

Explore who you are. Don't compare. Take responsibility for making the best of your life.

Wise, wise words.

Remember the secret? God wants to make you more like Jesus through your family life. Well, your older brothers and sisters can play big roles in that. How?

- Watch them.
- Mirror the good things you see.
- Distance yourself from character qualities, decisions, and philosophies that *aren't* God's best for you.
- Shrug it off when others compare you to them. (And try not to *assume* they're comparing when they might not be.)
- Beware of secret clubs and nasty potions. Just sayin'.
- Be you!

God, I realize that a lot of girls wish they had older brothers and sisters, so thank You for mine. Sometimes I get frustrated with the comparisons people make. Other times I feel like I just don't measure up. But I know You've made me unique. Help me see myself the way You see me. Show me how to be my own person. And help me learn from my siblings' successes and mistakes as I make my own path in life—a path headed toward You, Father. I ask these things in Jesus' name. Amen.

Application Questions

1. What funny memories do you have of trying to earn your older siblings' acceptance?

2. What expectations of you do others have that are based on your older siblings' personalities, performance, and interests?

3. *How do you deal with those expectations and comparisons?*

4. *What comparisons do you make between yourself and your older siblings?*

5. *Do you sometimes resent your older siblings because of the expectations others have for you because of them? If so, do you have any ideas how you could avoid resentment?*

6. *Think about the choices your older siblings have made and the way they have lived their lives. Write down at least three qualities or choices that would be good for you to imitate:*

Now write down at least three of their qualities or choices that you want to improve on:

7. *What are some healthy ways you can (or do) show that you are an original?*

CHAPTER EIGHT

The Family Feud

HAVE WE BEEN friends long enough now for me to share one of my biggest and least publicly known weaknesses? It's not something I'm exactly *proud* of, and actually I feel a little embarrassed to share it. But this moral failure of mine has everything to do with what we're going to talk about in this chapter, and I want to make sure you know at the outset that I am *not* perfect. I'm as human, passionate, and sinful as the next girl when it comes to family fights. I'm still a work in progress too.

I'm a thrower.

It doesn't happen often, and now that I think about it, there is only one person on the planet who can get me mad enough to chuck things. (I love you, honey!) I'm usually quite even-tempered, but sometimes I have this limit to my patience—a kind of threshold—and once it's crossed, anything within reach is liable to get flying lessons.

Maybe a pot of oatmeal.

Or an open bag of chips.

Once it was my cell phone.

Most shamefully, I sent God's Holy Word flying through the air. (I wish I were joking!)

Ironically, the handful of times I've gotten mad enough to throw something in anger, our fight came to a screeching halt. I, horrified by my outburst, would collapse into a ball of sorriness and tears on the floor, and he (for some reason I can't quite understand) would find me kind of cute in my miserable regret and let the offense go. (He's kind of the best.) Whatever made us so mad was forgotten as we cleaned up a mess of sticky oats off the stove or put the pieces of my cracked phone back together.

Like I said, it's not something I'm proud of, and I can tell you that my outbursts of anger never *solve* anything (even if they have brought an odd, temporary truce). So I'm working on it. In fact, I haven't thrown anything in a long(ish) time now. (Yay!)

The point is, when more than one hot-blooded person lives under the same roof, conflicts are bound to happen. We get under each other's skin. We misunderstand and we're misunderstood. We get grumpy and lazy in the way we talk. We put ourselves first. We disagree about freedom, trust, Internet use, and attitude. And because conflict is inevitable, we'd be wise to work on the way we fight so we can be catalysts of peace in our homes.

Let's face it: It's easier to yell, hit, ignore, and avoid conflict than it is to practice good communication. But I want more than that for you. As followers of Jesus, we know there's a better way to live than to just sit in our conflict, frustration, and hurt. It takes effort, time, and the Holy Spirit's help, but it *is* possible to have a disagreement without destroying the bonds of a family.

Have you ever chewed on the fact that Jesus was part of a family? A family, I might add, that was *not* perfect like He was? (Talk about being compared to a "perfect" older sibling!) I'd be willing to bet they had their share of family fights. Why? Because Jesus—and His family members—felt emotions. We see examples in Scripture of times Jesus disagreed with His family (see Matthew 12:46-50; John 2:3-4), worried His parents (see Luke 2:41-50), and got mad and sad (see John 2:13-17; 11:32-36). The Bible doesn't tell us much about Jesus' family life, but it sure makes it clear that He had human emotions much like you and I have. Yet Jesus found a way to grow through the conflicts He had; He was obedient to God, even while living in a flawed family.

I believe that's what He wants for us, as followers of Jesus, too. That's what this chapter is about. I want to give you some tips for "fighting fair" with your family, which will help you get better at communicating how you feel and dealing with others' feelings as well.

Communication 101

> **communication** (kə-myü-nə-'kā-shən) *noun*—a
> process by which information is exchanged between
> individuals; a technique for expressing ideas
> effectively (as in speech)[8]

The first key to avoiding unnecessary fights is simply to get better at communicating with a level head. According to that little definition I just gave, communication allows us to share what's on our minds and helps us understand what someone else is thinking and feeling. For example, you might tell your parents about all your wonderful, trustworthy attributes so they'll trust you enough to let you stay out past curfew. But—here's the important part—according to the definition, your mom and dad don't have to *agree* with you in order for communication to take place. Communication is the exchange of ideas and feelings—a way to hear and be heard. When we look at it that way, communication becomes a way to understand each other better instead of just a way to get what we want. As we mature, we should be able to come away from a discussion satisfied that we have been heard rather than fight tooth and nail until we get our way. Make sense?

As we grow up and start itching for more independence, it's only natural that some of our conversation time will revolve around trying to talk our parents into things. But do you want to know a secret? This is hard-won information, so use it wisely: You'll be more likely to "win" an argument with your parental unit if you don't *treat* it like an argument. As you communicate more like an adult (a mature adult, because . . . *um* . . . not all adults communicate like adults!), your parents will be more apt to treat you like one.

The book of Proverbs has a ton of great advice for communicating wisely as well as some harsh warnings against foolish talk. Here's a chart I've put together from Proverbs 12 that compares wise and foolish communication.

A Foolish Girl	A Wise Girl
Hates when others tell her she's wrong (verse 1)	Appreciates it when others show her where she's wrong because it makes her wiser (verse 1)
Gets trapped by (and frustrates others with) a rebellious attitude (verse 13)	Gets out of trouble with her honorable, cooperative attitude (verse 13)
Insists, "My way is right" (verse 15)	Really listens to others to see if they might be right (verse 15)
Gets irritated easily and lets everyone know she's mad (verse 16)	Lets insults slide and doesn't take it personally if others don't agree with her (verse 16)
Twists or exaggerates the truth to make a point (verse 17)	Only tells the truth, and in a loving way (verse 17)
Stabs people with careless, mean words (verse 18)	Uses her words to bless others and help them heal (verse 18)
Plans ways to hurt others or create drama (verse 20)	Finds joy in spreading peace (verse 20)

I don't know about you, but I think I'll be working on "wise" communication for the rest of my life. Sheesh! It sure doesn't come naturally, does it? I mean, who likes to admit when someone else is right, let alone be told when we're wrong? But if we can get a handle on those seven qualities of wise communication—man, what a beautifully *different* way to shine the love of Jesus to our family, even in the middle of a disagreement.

Look, when I'm mad, I'm at my worst. When I don't get my way or don't feel like I'm being treated well, that's hands down the *hardest* time to reflect Christ. If God wants to use our families to make us more like Jesus, then a conflict is like the "big game," where you get to see if all your hard work (Bible study, prayer, and so on) has actually made you a better player. It's like the dance recital where you have to leave everything onstage. I can't think of a better (or harder!) situation to show patience, honor, and selflessness than in the middle of a conflict. And that's exactly why it's worth working on.

As we get better at communicating, we'll be more likely to avoid all-out fights with our family members—which, according to these gems, is a big win:

> Starting a quarrel is like opening
>   a floodgate,
>   so stop before a dispute breaks out.
>
> PROVERBS 17:14

> Avoiding a fight is a mark of honor;
>   only fools insist on quarreling.
>
> PROVERBS 20:3

Remember, disagreements are bound to happen. So how can we practice good communication in the middle of a heated moment at home? How can we fight fair so that our disagreements don't lead to full-fledged war? I've got six tips for that. (Just so we're clear, throwing things will not be one of them.) I think you'll see that as you and your family practice these tips, it's possible to leave an argument feeling *at peace*, knowing that you've heard, you've been heard, and everyone still loves each other.

Six Tips for Avoiding a Big Fight

Tip #1: Stay Humble

If you're going to avoid World War III, you have to start with a humble heart. This tip is numero uno for a reason: You're going to need a big dose of humility to practice tips 2 through 6.

Humility means having a modest or realistic view of one's own importance. Jessie's definition? A humble girl understands that the world doesn't revolve around her and treats others the way she wants to be treated (even when she's hurt or mad) because she honors them (even if they don't "deserve" it). Easier said than done, right? Humility takes practice and one *big* work of the Holy Spirit in our hearts! That's why this tip is one you'll have to work on *before* a conflict takes place. You'll need a heart full of it so that when you get "bumped," only sweetness and grace spill out.

Tip #2: Focus on One Issue at a Time

Let's say you're working on a big paper for school. You sit down at your computer to do some research and open your Internet browser of choice. Hidden in that little search field lies an online world / virtual maze filled with more detours, distractions, and waylays than the Land of Oz. If you don't stay focused on the *reason* you sat down, you can easily waste two hours catching up on the latest Hollywood drama, watching random pet videos, and browsing five hundred pins of cute clothes and beauty tips that rarely work in real life—everything *other* than the research you sat down to do!

The same is true in a family conflict. If you don't stay focused on what you're trying to accomplish (that core issue you're trying to resolve), you can easily get sidetracked by unrelated irritations and side conflicts that were never the real problem. For example, let's say you're trying to persuade your mom to buy you a new phone for Christmas. You might begin by explaining why the newer model of phone is a *way* better product than the phone you have. But if you don't stay focused on that issue, it could easily lead to hurt feelings when you insist your mom's not cool enough to know that your phone is obsolete, which might then spiral into how you never show respect to your mom, which then might lead to the assumption that you just don't understand each other and that your mom doesn't trust you and you need a new family. These things happen.

On the other hand, if you stay focused on one issue at a

time, you can make your request, hear your mom's answer, maybe add a piece or two of info she may not have considered, and then *move on.* It's simple and freeing when we don't let the core issue "spaghetti" into a bunch of tangled issues.

Tip #3: Choose Your Words Wisely

Like the chart we looked at on page 145, a foolish girl pays no attention to the words she says. When she's angry, she just blurts out whatever comes to mind. A wise girl, on the other hand, "thinks carefully before speaking" (Proverbs 15:28).

Certain words and phrases do more harm than good in a disagreement. Words such as *never* and *always* ignite emotion (e.g., "You never listen!" or "You always take her side!"). You'll get nowhere fast with insults, low blows, and accusations. They put the other person on the defensive and sabotage your chances of actually being heard. Not only will you ruin your chances of getting your points across, but you can also do serious damage to relationships that could otherwise bless you.

Oh, and *not saying anything?* That can be just as hurtful and frustrating in an argument. Deciding to give the silent treatment to prove you're unhappy or that you're in control is no more helpful than yelling and screaming.

So tell the truth, share your feelings, and ask questions, but choose your words carefully. Let them drip with 1 Corinthians 13–style love, coated with patience, kindness, forgiveness, selflessness, and hope.

Tip #4: Control Your Emotions

Controlling one's emotions in the middle of an argument is downright hard! (Hence my airborne cell phone.) Sometimes tears well up or tempers flare and it takes everything in us to keep our feelings from spewing like a shaken soda can all over the people around us.

Proverbs 17:27 says, "A truly wise person uses few words; a person with understanding is even-tempered." When you're trying to work out a conflict, wild emotions can be your biggest enemy. Fiery feelings turn small disagreements into *big* drama. On the other hand, if you can keep a level head and humble heart, you'll be surprised how much you can accomplish.

For example, let's say you ask your parents if you can stay over at a friend's house, even though it's a school night. You have all sorts of reasons why it's a good idea, such as the fact that you could study with your friend for the history test you have tomorrow. If your parents say no and you throw attitude, raise your voice, or slam your bedroom door in a huff, you'll be three steps behind where you were before the discussion started. They're sure not going to change their minds after a blowup like that (can you blame them?), and next time they probably won't be likely to say yes either. On the other hand, if you can calmly hear out their reasons and accept their decision without going crazy, they'll be much more likely to trust you and give you the freedom you're hoping to earn.

Your parents are human too, remember. If your emotions start flaring up—if you raise your voice or make accusations—it's going to be hard for them not to fire back. One outburst ignites another, and it doesn't take long before everyone is piping mad at each other. Even if your parents get emotional first, do your best to keep your head on your shoulders so you can think clearly.

We talk a lot about Proverbs 15:1 around my house: "A gentle answer deflects anger, but harsh words make tempers flare." It's amazing how true this is! If we can somehow respond gently and quietly when someone comes at us with verbal guns ablazing, we can usually end a big argument before it starts. A gentle answer puts out a temper like water on a campfire. If you can keep your emotions in check, you can stop a discussion from escalating into an emotional sparring match.

Tip #5: Use Toy Swords

Speaking of sparring, in our family feuds, we should never use "deadly" weapons. In fact, our fights should look more like two kids playing with plastic swords than warriors fighting to the death with steel blades.

Obviously, we should never use *real* weapons against our family members, whether fists, nails, teeth, baseball bats, trophies, cosmetic bags, or—sigh—Bibles. But words can also seriously injure their targets. Proverbs 15:4 says, "Cutting words wound and maim" (MSG).

What sorts of words have the ability to make others bleed? Here are some "lethal weapons" to avoid:

- Criticizing something the other person can't change, such as her appearance or his learning ability.

- Bringing up a person's past mistakes or things you've already forgiven.
- Cussing or coarse language.
- Degrading someone's identity, such as telling her she is worthless or you hate her.
- Threatening to hurt the other person, emotionally or physically.

Man, those kinds of words cut deep! And they are *really* hard to forget, so they can keep wounding over and over as the person remembers them even years down the road. So let's make a pact to ban deadly weapons from our fights. Deal?

Tip #6: Call a Truce

Sometimes we can go round and round a subject and still not be any closer to a resolution, especially if you and your fam have wills of iron. (Stubborn? *Me?*) Maybe there are certain topics and scenarios that your family just can't seem to agree on, no matter how many times you try. In those situations, there comes a point when you have to call a truce to preserve your sanity, preferably before you do serious damage to each other *or* to the house. There ain't no shame in calling uncle if continuing to hammer away at each other would do more harm than good. King Solomon understood this. That's why he said, "A brother offended is more unyielding than a strong city, and quarreling is like the bars of a castle" (Proverbs 18:19, esv).

When you're at a standoff—when you realize that neither of you is going to budge on your differing opinions—rather than bringing in the battering ram to break through the castle walls, agree to take some time to think things through and try talking about it again another time. Just taking some time to cool off can help you see more clearly and avoid a big fight.

Practice Makes Perfect

How 'bout we put all those great communication tips to the test? I'll describe a scenario based on some common arguments between parents and daughters, and then you decide the outcome.

SCENARIO #1: AT THE STROKE OF TEN

Caroline knows that if she gets home one minute after curfew, her car won't turn into a pumpkin or her dress into rags but she'll be grounded for a good two weeks. The problem is, she's with a bunch of friends and *really* wants to stay out. Being the good daughter she is, she decides to call her mom to ask permission (Mom's usually the more lenient one). But, *slightly* on purpose, Caroline decides to wait until ten minutes before curfew, knowing that it takes twenty minutes to drive home.

Her mom answers the phone, and Caroline explains the situation. "Can I *please* stay out just another half hour?" she pleads, in her best too-cute-to-refuse voice. But her mom, slightly annoyed that Caroline waited until ten minutes before curfew to ask, replies, "No, honey. I'd like you to leave now. And because you'll be late getting home, we'll talk about your consequences in the morning."

How should Caroline respond?

SCENARIO #2: A BOY AND HIS BOARD

Noelle met Josh at youth group about a month ago. She's had a crush on him ever since she first saw him, but up to this point, she wasn't sure if he returned her interest. This afternoon, though, after church, Josh asked Noelle if she wanted to watch his surf tournament next Saturday and afterward go to the movies. She can hardly stand it, she's so excited!

As soon as she gets home from church, she tells her parents her plans. But Dad is none too excited about the idea of them going to the movies alone together, especially since he and Mom don't really know Josh. So he says, "Sorry, pumpkin. You can go to the tournament with your friends, but if you want to spend time with Josh afterward, you can bring him over to the house."

How should Noelle respond?

SCENARIO #3: BATHROOM TROUBLES

Hope shares a bathroom with her two sisters. They have a set schedule for their morning routines, but when she gets up for school and her little sister is in the shower at *her* time and uses all the hot water, Hope is ticked. Now she won't get a shower before school. When Hope tries to talk to her sister about it, her little sis acts like it's no big deal.

How should Hope respond?

Now it's your turn. Describe a situation that might come up with your parents or siblings. Then write an ending that you think might be more productive than the same old way you usually try to get your point across. Good luck!

SCENARIO #4:

How should you respond?

The Kernel of Truth

I *love* popcorn. Years ago my mom bought me one of those old-fashioned popcorn makers as a housewarming gift, and I've never gone back to microwave popcorn since. The Whirley Pop might sound like a carnival ride, but it's the best thing to happen to corn in five thousand years. This is truth. I'd like to hug whoever thought of such a practical piece of equipment, because there's nothing like the smell of popping corn or the taste of a little fresh melted butter when it's hot off the stove. Hold on, I think I need to make a batch before I continue. For inspiration.

(Did you think I was joking? I just made myself a big ol' bowl!)

A dried kernel of corn doesn't look like much, does it? Certainly not very appetizing. It's so hard and dense, you could chip a tooth trying to eat it like that. But the fascinating thing about dried corn kernels—and the reason we can pop them and then eat them—is that each one contains a *tiny* bit of moisture tucked away inside. It's not much. In fact, the only way we know there's moisture inside is because of what happens when we turn up the heat. As the kernel heats up, that tiny bit of moisture turns into gas and expands and expands until there's so much pressure on the walls of the kernel that it can't take it anymore. *Pop!* In a violent explosion (think about how scary it would be to an ant if he happened to be next to a kernel when it blew), all the insides force their way out and we have the airy, crunchy deliciousness we all love—all because of a little H_2O hidden away in a hard exterior.

I suppose it's time to explain what popcorn has to do with family feuds. Here's the point: Sometimes the things a parent, brother, or sister says when we're in the middle of a family fight contain a *tiny* bit of truth about us hidden in a rough exterior. That truth might be that we really do have a bit of attitude or we really weren't completely truthful or we really were a bit selfish. Just like the moisture in the kernel of corn, usually we never know that those little uglies exist until someone "turns up the heat" on us.

God has a way of speaking to us through other people. In the heat of emotions, we tend to brush off anything and everything the other person says, but we'll be better people if we can learn to accept those tiny bits of truth and grow from them. If you're arguing with your parents because they don't trust you to do something that you really want to do, you might ask yourself, *Is there any way I've been untrustworthy?* If your sister complains that you're being mean to her, really consider whether you have been unkind or unloving lately.

Proverbs 15:31 reminds us of the value of this: "If you listen to constructive criticism, you will be at home among the wise." Our natural (um, sinful) tendency is to get angry when someone points out a flaw. But we'll belong with the wise crowd if we listen to constructive criticism. So let's ask God to open our minds to any kernels of truth that He may want to show us through our family feuds and then accept that correction with grace.

Over the next week, when you have discussions or disagreements with your family and friends, look for the kernels of truth: those things you need to work on in your own life. Write your findings in your journal and ask God to help you work on those uglies. I'll be doing the same about myself.

I hope this chapter has given you a jump start in learning how to communicate (and even disagree) while still keeping your cool. A levelheaded girl has a much greater chance of winning her parents' trust and her siblings' respect. And most of all, she makes God proud as she becomes more like Christ.

Dear God, You and I both know that conflicts are hard for me. I want to be able to control my emotions—fear, anger, hurt, disrespect—but I can do it only with Your help. Help me get better at self-control. Make me more like Jesus: through Your Word, Your Spirit inside me, and even my parents' and siblings' comments—so that I can be an agent of peace in my family. Amen.

Application Questions

1. *How do arguments in your family usually end? How do you wish they'd end?*

2. *Have you ever had a fight with a family member that actually accomplished something? Do you think it's possible?*

3. *Taking an honest look at the way you act and the words you say during an argument, would you consider yourself part of the problem or part of the solution? What can you do personally to help your family's disagreements be more productive?*

4. *What percentage of the conversations you have with your parents center on trying to get them to see things your way (as opposed to just talking about life, the weather, your relationships with God, your favorite sports teams, and so on)?*

5. *On a scale of 1 to 10, how good are you at controlling your emotions in the middle of a disagreement, with 1 being "ice-cold" and 10 being "hot-blooded"?*

    1   2   3   4   5   6   7   8   9   10

6. *Now that you've read the six tips for avoiding a big fight, do you think it's possible to have a family disagreement that actually accomplishes something? Why or why not?*

7. *Which of the six rules does your family already do pretty well?*

8. *Which of the six rules do you need to practice? (You can list more than one!)*

9. *Would you say you have a teachable heart? Do you look for the kernel of truth in your arguments and accept correction from family members gracefully?*

CHAPTER NINE

Daddy's Little Girl

I watch the red-orange Chicago sun cast long shadows
over the freeway. The anticipation sends my stomach
into knots. So many questions left unanswered. I am
determined to be myself—only me. No tricks; no
efforts to be more than I am. The past is just that, and
the future is held in the setting Chicago sun.

WRITTEN JUST BEFORE MEETING STEVE,
THURSDAY, SEPTEMBER 18, 1997

I was seventeen the day I met my biological father. I entered
the fancy Italian restaurant where my mom, sister, and I were
to meet him, stuffing down a lifetime of questions I had never
asked, determined to just be me. A tall, handsome man in a
dark suit and tie strode up and asked with a grin, "Someone
I know?" His confidence and warmth put me at ease right
away. I nodded and smiled. He held out his hand, which I
shook. "Hi, I'm Steve," he said in a deep, friendly voice.

This was *him*—the man I had wondered about for as long

as I could remember. The man who gave my mom the glass terrarium I kept on my shelf, which was the only thing—other than my DNA—that linked me to him. I tried to look casual. Calm. Cool. None of which I actually felt.

Four days earlier, before we left on the cross-country trip that included this quick but fateful stop in Chicago, I had spilled my guts onto lined paper, giving voice to the pain, confusion, and questions that I had been too afraid to ask all those years of childhood.

Questions

I don't have the answers to all of life's questions.
I don't know what happened to make you leave.
Or were you ever there at all?
I don't know if it was hard for you—
Always wondering, never knowing,
What became of the little girl you created.
I don't know if you spent sleepless nights wondering
What color her eyes were,
Where she played make-believe.
Did you ever shed tears
Knowing she had nobody to call Daddy?
Did you care?
Have you ever watched a young lady and wondered if she
*   resembles you?*
Is she beautiful or plain?
Tall? Short?

Adventurous or scared?
Are you afraid she resents you for time not spent,
Doing the things most fathers do with their daughters?
Do you ever wish you had been there—
Through her first words,
Her first day of kindergarten,
Her first kiss,
Her first broken heart?
I don't know if you ever wish you could go back in time
and do things differently.
Do you regret decisions made?
Or has time borne forgetfulness?

At the time, they were questions I didn't know if I'd ever get answers to, about a man I couldn't even picture.

Now we sat across a table from each other: a seventeen-year-old senior and the man who gave her life. He and my mom made small talk about Chicago, his family, bratwurst, and Harleys. The nonchalance of the conversation was frustrating and soothing at the same time. Every once in a while, I'd catch him staring at me. His dimples showed when he smiled. I liked that.

As dinner wound down, he said that he was surprised to hear from my mom and asked what made me want to come see my "old man" after all these years. I don't remember what I said. Whatever it was, it didn't come close to the whole truth. There was no way to put words to five hundred emotions at once. How could I explain to him that there's a part of a girl that feels tied to her father, whether he's been in her life or not? How could I explain the battle that had gone on in my heart—wanting so badly to have a relationship with the man whose DNA I shared but not wanting to slight my stepdad (the man who had *chosen* to love me) by making contact with him? There were just no words for all that.

After dinner, Steve took me for a drive to the edge of town in his little black sports car, just the two of us. With the top down, the full moon gave his face a silvery glow, deepening my suspicions that this whole ordeal was actually a dream. We talked about life, my college plans, and his once-upon-a-time college struggle. He gave me advice about following my dreams and not trying to please everyone with my life choices. I felt completely at ease, as though I had known him forever, not the mere hour and a half that had passed. Too soon, we got to the off-ramp where I would be getting back into my mom's car for the last leg of the trip. His long, tight hug assured me that I wasn't the only one feeling emotions that night. Tears stung the corners of my eyes as he kissed the top of my head, and we said good-bye. Seventeen years of wondering, fearing, hoping, praying—*over*. The night felt a bit magical—a gift from God to a girl who was getting ready to make her way in the world.

Tell Me I'm Beautiful

Mind if I ask you a question? What do you think about a dad's role? I mean, how would you define his job as it relates to his kids?

About a half dozen roles come to my mind, but there's one in particular I think is worth mentioning.

If you've read my book *Backwards Beauty*, this truth should ring a bell: As girls, we have a desire to be desirable; in other words, *we want to be wanted*. We want to know that we're beautiful and "worth it"—that we're worthy of a man's love. When a family is healthy, the first man to confirm a girl's worth and beauty like that is her dad. If it weren't for that annoying sin nature—our fallen spirit as humans because of what went down in Genesis 3—a daddy would *always* make a girl feel protected and help her understand what true love looks like. She would gain confidence in his love, which would help her know what to look for in a romantic relationship when she grew up. She would have a standard by which she could measure any guy who caught her eye. She could ask herself, *Does my hot new crush treat me with the same love, devotion, care, respect, and gentleness that my daddy does?* And if not, she wouldn't give a second thought to ditching that guy.

Does a dad take on that role? Sometimes. But sadly, most girls don't have that kind of father figure in their lives. They don't have strong, steady men who walk with them from childhood to adulthood, confirming their worth and helping them know just how beautiful, capable, and strong they are. I wish that weren't so. I wish *every* girl had the chance to feel that kind of love! Because ultimately a dad's role is supposed to be a reflection of our heavenly Daddy's love for us. Your dad's love should be the first taste you get of the unconditional, uplifting, unyielding love God has for you.

But here we are in the real world.

No matter how "good" a dad is, he *can't* be perfect. Because humans are sinners by nature, he's simply not capable of it—which means that to one degree or another, we daughters are going to have to learn to make wise choices and become our true selves without depending on our earthly dads to form our characters. We need a bigger, stronger, more stable Daddy for that. A Daddy who *can*, *will*, and *has* confirmed our beauty, ability, and strength. A Daddy who loves with unconditional, uplifting, unyielding love. A Daddy who knows everything about us and cares about our hurts, hearts, dreams, and desires.

There's only one Daddy I know of who fits that job description:

> Even before he made the world, God loved us and chose us in Christ to be holy and without fault in his eyes. God decided in advance to adopt us into his own family by bringing us to himself through Jesus Christ. This is what he wanted to do, and it gave him great pleasure. So we praise God for the glorious grace he has poured out on us who belong to his dear Son. EPHESIANS 1:4-6

> And because we are his children, God has sent the Spirit of his Son into our hearts, prompting us to call out, "*Abba*, Father." GALATIANS 4:6, EMPHASIS ADDED

Our heavenly Daddy knows the best gifts to give us (see Matthew 7:11; James 1:17) and the best ways to correct us (see Proverbs 3:11-12), and He replaces our fear with an understanding of our true worth and beauty through His Spirit (see Romans 8:15). I think we'd better read each one of those verses, just to make sure we get this down deep:

> So if you sinful people know how to give good gifts to your children, how much more will your heavenly Father give good gifts to those who ask him.
> MATTHEW 7:11

> Whatever is good and perfect is a gift coming down to us from God our Father, who created all the lights in the heavens. He never changes or casts a shifting shadow.   JAMES 1:17

> My child, don't reject the LORD's discipline, and don't be upset when he corrects you. For the LORD corrects those he loves, just as a father corrects a child in whom he delights.   PROVERBS 3:11-12

> So you have not received a spirit that makes you fearful slaves. Instead, you received God's Spirit when he adopted you as his own children. Now we call him, "Abba, Father."   ROMANS 8:15

Trust me, I know exactly how deep daddy-hurts cut into our hearts. I'm not preaching at you from some Cinderella castle in the sky, patting your little head like a kind schoolmarm. I've been in the trenches with this stuff, and I'm choosing my next words very carefully: God can heal your hurts, encourage your strengths, and fill up all the gaps your dad left in your heart when he left you (physically or emotionally). And God can use the imperfect efforts of any dad in your life—whether biological, step-, foster, or adopted—to make you more than who you are today. You just have to let Him.

I know this. *I've lived this.*

The Letdown

My surreal night in Chicago was the start of a short-lived connection with my biological father. Steve and I wrote letters back and forth for a year or so. I told him about my transition to college, volleyball, and random happenings, and he shared about his transition away from a company he started, family vacations, and his love for motorcycles. But one day my letters stopped getting replies. Several attempts to reach out over the years have gone unanswered. After what seemed to be a dream reunion, I was left once again with nothing but questions: *What happened? Did I say something wrong? Was I not worth the effort of a relationship?*

Questions like that can haunt us. When dads (or moms or siblings) abandon us, it's so tempting to look at ourselves and ask, *What's wrong with* me? Does blaming ourselves or questioning our worth do one iota of good? Nope. Because the problem *isn't* us. That's just what Satan—who is also a father, the father of *lies* (see John 8:44)—would like us to believe. He knows that if you or I let someone else's wrong choices define our core identities, we'll never become the warrior chicks God intends us to be. We'll be too busy licking our family wounds to notice the epic spiritual battle going on all around us.

Once again, this no-nonsense truth plays out: When it comes to the hard stuff in life, God doesn't excuse us from living His way. Was it unfair that your dad left you, hurt you, neglected you, or didn't value you the way he should have? Absolutely. But is it possible to rise above your pain and grab hold of the truth about who you *really are* because of what your Father God has done for you? Yes, yes, and yes!

Sis, finding your identity, worth, and value not in an imperfect dad but in a perfect and loving Father is the best thing you can do for yourself. You are not defined by your dad with a lowercase *d*; you're made new by your Dad with a big ol' whopping uppercase *D*! *Please* don't let Satan use your past or present sucky circumstances to steal your joy, confidence, hope, or future. Instead, let God fill you up.

Already Full

As a girl who knows the pain of abandonment, the sting of rejection, and the fallout from sinful family relationships, let me give it to you straight: You can either feel bad for yourself because of what you *don't* have—memories, stability, warmth, security—or you can choose to let God fill those broken places with His life-giving Spirit. If you'll let God be your Daddy—if you'll get to know Him, rely on Him, learn from Him, and see yourself through His eyes—there's nothing in this life you won't be able to overcome.

Psalm 68:5-6 says,

> Father to the fatherless, defender of widows—
>> this is God, whose dwelling is holy.
> God places the lonely in families;
>> he sets the prisoners free and gives them joy.

God Himself is a father to the fatherless, a mother to the motherless, a sibling to the only child. But we have to open our eyes and see just how full we already are in Christ.

When you were a little girl, did you ever have one of those magic baby bottles for your dolls? Mine was pink, and when I held it upright, it looked full of "milk" for my doll, but when I tipped it upside down to feed my baby, it quickly emptied as the baby "drank" it. (No small thang to a three-year-old!) The "magic" was that there was never actually any more or less liquid in the bottle. Whether it was "empty" or "full" was all a matter of perspective. It just depended on which way the bottle was tipped.

Too many people go through life with their bottles upside down. They look at their family situations and all they see is "empty" because their dads aren't around, or their parents fight, or their brothers are in jail. And from a human perspective, empty really is all they've got. But if they could see things from God's perspective for a minute, they'd see that their bottles—their lives—were full all along. Joy, peace, security, confidence—they're all right there for the taking, in plain sight. We just have to tip the bottle back up, so to speak, and look at life from a different perspective. We have to see our story with spiritual eyes.

Here's the most beautiful part in all of this. When God fills us up, we can offer instead of take. Family relationships add to our joy, but a lack of them can't steal our peace. We can see our beauty and worth even if no one else in the family does. We can live life without an earthly dad (or live *with*

I know letting God "fill you up" might sound mystical or churchy to you right now, but I promise that if you make it your life's goal to get close to God, He won't disappoint. He's not playing some cosmic game of hide-and-seek, waiting in some hard-to-reach corner until you finally run across His hiding spot. He wants to be found!

> "For I know the plans I have for you," says the LORD.
> "They are plans for good and not for disaster, to give you a future and a hope. In those days when you pray, I will listen. *If you look for me wholeheartedly, you will find me.*"
> Jeremiah 29:11-13, emphasis added

If you need some practical places to start looking for God "wholeheartedly," come find me at www.LifeLoveandGod.com/deeper.

---

an imperfect one), because those who trust in Yahweh lack *nada. Zilch. Nothing.*

> Even strong young lions sometimes go hungry,
>> but those who trust in the LORD will lack no good
>> thing.
>
> PSALM 34:10

Do you believe it, sis?

I don't think my and Steve's story is finished yet, by the way. I haven't had any luck making contact with him in the years since college, but I'm holding on to hope. God specializes in unexpected twists to even the most seemingly predictable stories. The beautiful thing, though, is that I'm not *missing* anything in my heart. If I do get the chance to rekindle a relationship with Steve, I won't be expecting him to do something for me that he simply can't do. Instead, I'll just have lots extra of God's love overflowing from my heart, which I can share with him and his family.

Okay, before we bring this chapter to a close, let's zoom out and take a look at the big picture. If the whole point of family life is to make us more like Jesus Christ, what can we take away here? I mean, Jesus' Dad (God) was *perfect* (lucky Him). How can we become more like Jesus if it doesn't seem as though our dads are living up to their God-given roles?

It's true: Jesus' Dad (God) *is* perfect. But Jesus had an earthly dad too, remember? And even though we don't know a ton about Joseph, we do know one thing with 100 percent

certainty: he *wasn't* perfect. And check this out: Bible schol-
ars believe that Joseph died in Jesus' teens or twenties. Jesus
knew what it meant to live with an imperfect dad, and He
probably knew what it felt like to live without one. In both
situations, Jesus allowed God to be His source of comfort,
instruction, worth, and validation. No matter what His
earthly dad was or was not contributing to His life, Jesus
fulfilled His destiny, and we can too.

Instead of crying on a boyfriend's shoulder, self-
destructing, or walling up our hearts like the fortress of
Jericho, we can take our pain to God and let Him soften,
teach, and mend our hearts in ways only He can. The choice
of how you'll deal with your daddy-hurts is yours, and *only*
you can make it. Let's pray together that you'll make the right
one, shall we?

*Daddy—thank You for letting me call You that, by
the way. I know it breaks Your heart to see the way sin
has ripped apart the loving family relationships You
designed for life on earth. There's something in me that
longs so much to feel my earthly dad's love! I know
that's not wrong, but I also know that he has and will
let me down sometimes and that our relationship won't
last forever. So I want to put all my hope in You, God.
I want to find my worth, beauty, confidence, and joy
in You. Please, be my everything. And help me show
unconditional love to my dad, even when he doesn't
deserve it. I love You so much! Amen.*

Application Questions

1. How would you describe your relationship with the dad(s) in your life?

2. What kind of connection do you think there is between a girl's relationship with her dad and her view of her beauty, worth, and abilities?

3. If your relationship with your dad is rocky, how has that affected your life, decisions, and other relationships (particularly with guys)?

4. Do you think it's possible to allow God to be your source of comfort, instruction, worth, and validation? What are a few practical ways you could allow Him to do that?

5. Whether we are missing out or have enough is often a matter of perspective. In your life, would you say you've been viewing your "bottle" as empty or full? What are three practical ways you can view your life as full, even if your relationship with your dad isn't what you wish it was?

CHAPTER TEN

It Won't Always Be This Way

I HAD A better-than-average relationship with my mom growing up. Maybe it goes back to those first five years when it was just the two of us. Or maybe it's simply that kids are drawn to genuine love like a kitten to milk. No matter how old I got or how hormonal or how distracted with freedom and friends, my heart was knit together with hers.

Of course, we still hurt each other. We had our share of hard days when tempers flared and eyes rolled (both usually mine). We said words we wished we could take back. I can still hear the echo of my bedroom door slamming in the hallway of many teen memories. We had fights for dumb reasons. But when I think about the years I spent at home, it's not the fights I regret most; it's the *indifference*. Looking back, too often I took the relationship I had with my mom (and dad and siblings) for granted.

When we're teens—distracted by drama, blindly boy crazy, or intoxicated with independence—we don't really think much about how change will eventually, well, *change* things. At least I didn't. I don't remember ever thinking about the fact that I wouldn't always come home from school to my mom's big hug and her listening ear. My days wouldn't always end with her rubbing my back and asking about my day while I lay cozily in bed. Life wouldn't always give us the chance to take long road trips together or watch the seven-hour version of *Pride and Prejudice* on our sagging couch with a big bowl of popcorn (extra butter) between us. In fact, she wouldn't always be such a central part of my life. And if I had realized how much I would miss those moments, I would have savored them more. I would have enjoyed them the way I relish the memory of them now.

It's not that I thought life would go on the same way forever. I mean, I knew life would change. I was looking forward to it! I loved my mom dearly, but freedom was up ahead, calling to me like a siren. So I spent more time thinking about the future—college and guys and traveling the world—than savoring the moments I had with her.

Change Changes Things

For me, change came slowly and then all at once.

First, there was moving away to college. I became less

connected with home, little by little, with each passing month on my own. Years passed and I didn't always come home for the holidays. Then I got married, which naturally changed the amount of time I could spend with my mom, dad, and siblings.

And the change kept coming.

One morning I lay on a hospital bed while a nice technician rubbed my stomach with a cold, slimy gel and then rolled an ultrasonic transducer all over my growing baby bump.

A girl.

We were having a girl!

Of course I was ecstatic. I was going to have a daughter, just like my own momma. *Mom*—I couldn't wait to tell her.

Just as I guessed, she was beyond excited when I told her the news. I could hear it in her voice, which had been unusually tired lately. She was thrilled at the thought of having a granddaughter.

But she had been to the hospital that day too, to check on some symptoms she had been having, and she had to share some news of her own—news that would bring changes no one saw coming.

She had cancer.

I've always thought my mom was beautiful, inside and out. I remember hoping to look like her, when her long, brown hair began to gray just a little and the smile lines settled lovely at the corners of her eyes. I remember the smell of her favorite Clinique perfume on church mornings and special nights out. Even at a young age, I hoped someday I could love others the way she did: that selfless kind of love that motivated her to massage my grandpa's gnarled, neglected feet and trim his thick toenails. Or pick me up early from a dozen sleepovers because I couldn't shake homesickness. Or muck a horse stall all summer so I could take horseback-riding lessons. Or drive three hours for a hug after I'd had a hard day during my first year of college.

When I think of Mom, I think of smiles and spunk, friendliness, gentle wisdom, sarcasm, sacrifice, and gobs of grace. She had always been the kind of mom any daughter would be lucky to have—the type of woman I'd always wanted to be.

Not even the news of cancer could change that.

The next 246 days were the most bittersweet of my life. The excitement and anticipation for my coming daughter made my heart swell to match my belly. But even amid all that happiness, there was always a shadow of grief vignetting the corners of my mind as I watched my mom become thin and frail.

Mom lived life as fully as she could in the months that followed, as the fighter she had always been. Even though she was unnaturally cold and in constant pain, she came to my baby showers and drove four hours to welcome her grand-daughter into the world. She traveled out of state for my brother's wedding, though she could barely leave the hotel room. She wrote letters to her family, telling them about Jesus' love. She loved us and she loved her Savior till the end.

I was there, sitting on the floor at the foot of her bed, the morning she left her hollow body and stepped into eternity.

On September 7, 2007, at 7:07 a.m., *my momma was gone.*

I had spent as many days as I could with her in her final

months, but there was never enough time. Only in saying good-bye did I realize how much of the twenty-six good, healthy years we had together I had wasted. How many days living under the same roof had I taken for granted? That was time I could never get back.

Think about It

You and me, we need to think about death.

I'm not a pessimist; in fact, I'm a textbook optimist! But a wise girl thinks about how things will change in the future because it helps her appreciate the people she has today. Israel's wisest king, Solomon, understood this. He said,

> Better to spend your time at funerals than at parties.
> After all, everyone dies—
> so the living should take this to heart.
> Sorrow is better than laughter,
> for sadness has a refining influence on us.
> A wise person thinks a lot about death,
> while a fool thinks only about having a good time.

ECCLESIASTES 7:2-4

Now, I don't think Solomon meant that we should spend every Saturday morning jogging through a cemetery or watch only tearjerker documentaries. As with so many things in life, balance is key. Yet Solomon hints at a really profound secret in those verses: *The reality of death and change should make us live differently today.*

181

Rather than depress us, these verses challenge us to make the most of our time with our loved ones. They dare us to live with joy and purpose.

This is a book about learning to love our families, and one way we love well is to recognize that things won't always be as they are now. People die. Brothers move away for college or join the military. Sisters get married and start their own families. Grandparents become frail. You'll move out and make a life of your own.

When we're teenagers, it can be hard to fully grasp the impact those changes can have on us. We tend to live as though things will always be as they are. But the only thing I can predict for certain is that our lives *will not* stay as they are now. At some point, we will say *adios* to this season of being kids at home.

Of course, not all change is bad! For many, leaving home brings about some good and needed adjustments to the family scene.

I'll never forget coming home for Christmas after my first semester of college. Everything in my bedroom was exactly as I had left it—from my surf-picture-covered wall to my old wood desk—but it looked so strange, like I was looking at someone else's room or something. And it *smelled* different. (That's a change you don't expect.) But the thing that sticks out most about that first return home was the *peacefulness*. My family and I enjoyed each other's company in ways that we hadn't during most of my teen years. I didn't struggle with my attitude, and it was easier for all of us to be pleasant with each other and intentional about how we spent the time we had together.

Sometimes space does a relationship good. If things are hard at home right now, know that change can also bring healing and laughter to strained relationships. And sometimes just knowing that things will probably get better once you move out can help you focus on the positive aspects of family life today.

Whether the thought of change in your family makes you want to cry or shout for joy, how can you savor the time you have with your parents and siblings right now? How can you take advantage of all the positive aspects of family life while you have them? Well, it just so happens I have some ideas.

Living on Purpose

For most people, life just sort of *happens* to them. They don't give much thought about where they want to go and what they want their lives to look like. In their families, that means they just get by. They react to the people around them, but they don't think about the big picture—about how they want *to act* toward the people they love.

I want more for you than that. I want you to live your life—including your family life—on purpose. With a plan. On a mission. That's why I've put together the following "Family Manifesto." A manifesto is like a mission statement. I hope it will inspire you to make the most of the weeks, months, or years you have with the people you call family.

My Family Manifesto

I'll savor each day I have with my family, not knowing how many days I will get.

I'll record happy memories with my camera or journal so I can remember the good times.

I'll forgive quickly because life is too short to hold grudges.

I'll use my words to build up instead of tear down.

I'll be thankful for the sacrifices others make for me and tell them so.

I'll practice letting others choose/go first/have the final say instead of insisting on my own way.

I'll pray for my family members because—just like me—God has a plan for each of them.

I'll ask questions about their lives now because I may not always be able to.

I'll take time to just "be" together, without distractions.

I'll look for the good in my family members and tell them when I see it.

I'll try to stay calm even when I'm really upset.

When talking to friends, I'll be quick to point out my family's strong points instead of their weaknesses.

I'll set a good example for my siblings.

I'll tell my family I love them every chance I get.

I'll thank God for my family every day, even the hard days.

You can find a printable version of "My Family Manifesto" at www.LifeLoveandGod.com/family-manifesto.

Can you imagine what a difference it would make if we practiced this manifesto every day?

Life won't always go on the way it does right now, but when we live on purpose, we make the most of the time we do have with the people we love. And in the process, we squeeze all the sweetest juice out of life!

Hope like an Anchor

Change is normal. A lot of change is good. But some changes in our family can shake us to the core.

Cancer.

Jail time.

Suicide.

Divorce.

Yeah, some change feels like a freight train colliding with our chests. Maybe you already know what I'm talking about. Or maybe those kinds of changes haven't come into your life yet, and I'm glad. But I can't talk about change and living life on purpose without taking a moment to talk about how we can respond when those hard changes take place. I want to share something that carried me through my mom's sickness and can carry you through hard times too.

Death—or separation, or watching loved ones suffer—isn't the worst thing.

Life without God's hope is.

My mom knew exactly what would happen to her when she died. In fact, she had been looking forward to heaven—being face-to-face with Jesus—ever since she had become a Christ follower at thirty-one years old. When she was sick, one of her favorite Scripture portions was Job 19:25-26, written by a man who knew what it felt like to live in pain and sickness, on the brink of death. It says,

> But as for me, I know that my Redeemer lives,
>   and he will stand upon the earth at last.
> And after my body has decayed,
>   yet in my body I will see God!

As Christians, we know that this life isn't all there is. We have the hope that even if our loved ones don't know God when they die, He will work our suffering for good, to make us more like Christ (see Romans 8:28). And we have God's promise that He will comfort us in our deepest grief (see 2 Corinthians 1:3-5).

Hebrews 6:19 says, "This hope is a strong and trustworthy anchor for our souls."

An *anchor* for our souls.

Have you ever been sailing? I played around on a catamaran one summer, and though my nautical knowledge is pretty slim, I do understand the wind's power against a sail. (Said wind may have tipped my tiny vessel plumb over, dumping an embarrassed me right into the water—fully clothed.) A sailboat is at the mercy of the wind, waves, and currents of the ocean. If a powerful storm blows in, even a trained sailor can be helpless against it. God bless the person who invented anchors! An anchor does for a sailor what he can't do for himself: hold steady. Stay put. Ride out the storm. Having an anchor is the only way a boat can hold still on the constantly moving and changing surface of the water.

An anchored *soul*—now, that would be pretty revolutionary, don't you think?

The only reason I didn't shipwreck when I lost my mom to cancer is because my heart was anchored to God. I held steady when the waves crashed over my head because I knew the *hope* of the gospel.

I don't know what kind of life-altering changes you might face (or have faced) in your family. But I do know this: If hope anchors your soul, no storm will ultimately shipwreck you. That doesn't mean you won't feel as if your boat is breaking to bits from the force of the waves! But your faith has the ability to hold you steady when the storms hit. Notice I said

If you're facing (or have faced) a deep loss in your life, I recommend Elisabeth Elliot's excellent book *A Path through Suffering: Discovering the Relationship between God's Mercy and Our Pain.* My copy is thoroughly highlighted, scribbled in, and dog-eared.

when. Storms *will* hit, and some of them will hit hard. But God has promised to see you through (see Philippians 1:6), and He never goes back on His word. As long as you look to Him, your ship—your life—won't sink, even when life as you know it changes forever.

A Time to Live

When I was a kid, my parents usually played an oldies radio station in the car. We also spent a lot of time driving (because I kind of lived in the boondocks, remember). Those two facts combine to create a third, only slightly more interesting fact: I happen know the lyrics of just about every hit written in the fifties and sixties. Great use of brain space, I know.

So when I think about change, I start to hear music. More specifically, I hear this hippy-esque song covered by a band called the Byrds in the midsixties called "Turn! Turn! Turn!" Not only is it one of the few songs taken almost entirely from the Bible, but it also holds the distinction of being the number one hit with the oldest lyrics. How? Well, because the original writer happens to be King Solomon, that really wise guy who encouraged us to think about death. (I'm sure that obscure piece of trivia will come in handy someday. You're welcome.)

It isn't exactly the most melodic song. (But then I've never been a huge fan of folk-rock revolution/hippy tunes of the sixties.) The words are rather profound though, which, I suppose, is why they made a song out of them. Here's what Solomon wrote, taken from a more modern Bible translation:

For everything there is a season,
    a time for every activity under heaven.
A time to be born and a time to die.
    A time to plant and a time to harvest.
A time to kill and a time to heal.
    A time to tear down and a time to build up.
A time to cry and a time to laugh.
    A time to grieve and a time to dance.
A time to scatter stones and a time to gather stones.
    A time to embrace and a time to turn away.
A time to search and a time to quit searching.
    A time to keep and a time to throw away.
A time to tear and a time to mend.
    A time to be quiet and a time to speak.
A time to love and a time to hate.
    A time for war and a time for peace.

ECCLESIASTES 3:1-8

The point is, your life holds different seasons. Different times in our lives call for different perspectives.

So let me ask you something: Given that family life as you know it will change someday—maybe soon, maybe years from now—*what time is it?* The answer to that question is unique to you, your current season, and your family's dynamics. Is it time to heal? To grieve? To build others up? Is it time to celebrate, make peace, or speak up?

The answer to that question will help you make the most of the time you have with your family. Changes *will* come.

Why not go about your relationships in light of them? Love well. Live on purpose.

By the way, Jesus would have read and studied that passage in Ecclesiastes as a Jewish boy and then as a rabbi. I'm convinced He was always mindful of what "time" it was. I'm sure He made the most of every minute He had with His family—and then His disciples in those final years leading up to the Cross. Jesus knew there would be "a time to die," so He made the most of His time to live. I'm making it my mission to do the same. Will you join me?

> *God, thank You for the time You've given me with each person in my family. I want to make the most of what time we have together while we're under the same roof and while we're on the same earth. Help me know how to live now so that I won't have regrets later, when those changes come. Father, I know that change, separation, and death are parts of life, but the thought makes my heart ache. Please be my soul's anchor when devastating changes overwhelm me. Help me cling to You in the storm. Amen.*

Application Questions

1. How has your family changed since you were a little kid?

2. *What changes do you think might come in the next five to ten years? Does the thought of those changes scare or excite you?*

3. *How can the reality of death and change make us live differently today?*

4. *Pick three statements from "My Family Manifesto" (on page 184) to work on this week:*

5. *How can God's hope help anchor you in the big storms of family life?*

6. *Thinking about Ecclesiastes 3:1-8, what "time" do you think it is for you in your family?*

CHAPTER ELEVEN

A Family of Your Own

THE DAY I became Mrs. Minassian, I got a face full of cake to celebrate (and by "face full," I mean an entire layer of cake smeared all over my pristine makeup and meticulously curled hair. Yeah. You can see a picture of that epicness on the "Meet Jessie" page at www.LifeLoveandGod.com). In becoming a Minassian, though, I was also instantly joined to a pretty extraordinary family. I could go on and on about how much I appreciate Roger and Marilyn, my mother- and father-in-*love*, but I'll spare you the mushy stuff. Instead, I'll tell you a story about them so you can see what I've seen.

Roger had been a pastor for twenty-two years. He had a comfortable life with a comfortable job in a comfortable city.

But in 1992, after watching news reports of the Los Angeles riots, God stirred something in his heart. He wondered, *What kind of hopelessness makes kids burn their* own *neighborhoods?* He wept for the kids so ingrained in gang culture that they didn't know a better way to live or find justice, not just in LA but also in his own city of Fresno, California.

He wasn't sure what to do, but he knew that he had to do something.

At fifty-three years old, with Marilyn's unwavering support, this white pastor with no street smarts or gang experience left his comfortable church job and started a ministry called Hope Now For Youth. His vision was to offer hope to hopeless kids by giving them both a chance to hear the gospel and the skills they needed to get honest work. And it worked. Since 1993, Hope Now For Youth has placed more than two thousand former gang members into jobs, and Fresno—once the auto-theft capital of America—won an All-American City Award in 2000. The transformation was so inspirational that in 2014, a movie, *Finding Hope Now*, was made about Roger and Marilyn's story.

I told you, they're pretty amazing. But my point in sharing that story isn't just to brag about two of my favorite people. I mean, I'm always game for that, but I also want to share one of the most heartbreaking discoveries Roger made in the years he has worked with gang kids: Their families are usually a mess.

Broken homes.

Absent fathers.

Drugs, alcohol, anger, and abuse.

The stories of terrible family experiences became too common to ignore. Roger knew that if lasting cultural change was going to take place through generations, he had to teach the Hope Now students more than how to get a proper ID and interview for a job. He had to teach them how to change the family culture. He had to help them *end the cycle of brokenness* that pushed them to want to join gangs in the first place.

When you've grown up with dysfunction and it's all you really know, sometimes you can feel helpless to change it. Or maybe you vow that things will be different for your own family in the future, but without the skills to change, you go back to what you saw and heard modeled as a kid. That's why, at the beginning of the program, Roger gives this challenge to his students:

> I'll make you a promise. If you follow what I'm
> telling you to do and what the Lord wants you to
> do, your children will never have to go through what
> you've gone through.

Those two sentences are powerful. No one who has felt rejection, fear, pain, or neglect at the hands of their parents wants their own kids to walk the same road. To hear that *they don't have to* is good news indeed.

I don't know what your family situation is like. Maybe your family is stable and loving, or maybe it feels more like hell on earth. But even if you're facing what many of those gang kids were facing—abandonment, brokenness, abuse—I want you to know there's hope.

That cycle can stop here.

Your story doesn't have to be your kids' story.

Change isn't going to happen just because you hope it will, though. If you want to be the start of a new family legacy, you'll need to have a plan.

Reprogramming Brokenness

The former gang members Roger mentored had learned a certain way of behaving in a family. When they started attending the Hope Now For Youth program, they were already beginning to practice what they had learned from their fathers, and their new families were suffering for it. If Roger and his team hadn't intervened, the cycle would likely have continued in yet another generation.

You'll live what you learn—*unless you learn a new way.*

Just because as a kid you learned one way to do family doesn't mean you can't learn a new, better way to put into practice as an adult. That was the powerful message Roger gave to his students, and it's the hope I want to leave you with as we wrap up this book. Whether your current family is stable or broken, loves God or hates Him, is peaceful or rife with conflict, there is hope for the family *you* might have someday.

It can be downright scary for those who have been hurt by divorce or anger or addiction or any other pain to think that they might inflict the same pain on their future kids. I've talked to girls who are scared to get married and have children at all because they're afraid they'll repeat the same devastating mistakes their parents made. Maybe that's how you feel, or maybe you've never really thought about the effects your parents' or siblings' mistakes might have on how you live your future life. Either way, I have great news: You don't have to repeat history. Nobody and nothing will force you to make the same mistakes. You can have a healthy, functional, happy family no matter how messed up your current one is. Our God is a God of second chances, and He loves to rescue His children from less-than-ideal backgrounds and give them fresh starts.

> God, my God, I yelled for help
>   and you put me together.
> God, you pulled me out of the grave,
>   gave me another chance at life
>   when I was down-and-out.
>
> PSALM 30:2-3, MSG

God is in the business of reteaching broken people. Goodness, I'm living proof of that! Our part is to be teachable. Proverbs 16:20 says, "Those who listen to instruction will prosper; those who trust the LORD will be joyful."

God gives us instructions so we'll *prosper*, so we'll succeed in life! And when we trust Him—in every area of life, including the best way to do family—we'll find deep joy.

Success and *joy*. I'm guessing those are two things you want out of life too.

I can't tell you whether a family of your own is in your future. It's not like The Game of Life, in which you get a little blue man and a couple of plastic kids to put in your car just for playing the game. Nope—God doesn't promise that you'll get married or have kids. But don't you worry, 'cause thankfully those things aren't necessary to have a happy, meaningful life! (Remember, God cares most about two things: His glory and our good. Our "good" might not match what we *want*, but that's where we come to the whole "Trust the LORD" part of Proverbs 16:20, right?) So here's the deal: If marriage is God's best for you, He will bring you just the right man at just the right time. And if kids (biological or foster or adopted) are best for you or bring Him the most glory, they're a shoo-in too. You can trust Him with those details of your life because He's *for* you.

If marriage and children are part of God's perfect plan for your future, there are some other parts of God's will you can know for sure. Those parts are called God's "revealed will" because He shows us what they look like in His Word. Here's an example: If you get married, you know that God wants you to remain faithful to your spouse (see Exodus 20:14; Matthew 5:27-28) and to work on loving each other selflessly (see 1 Corinthians 13:4-7). If you have kids, you know that He wants you to spend time teaching them about the gospel (see Mark 16:15) and model God's way of living (see Deuteronomy 6:6-7).

We've talked about other parts of God's revealed will for

family life in this book too: forgiveness, honor and respect, trust, conflict resolution, leading by example, expressing love, and growing in holiness. You might think of this book as your course in "Family Life 101." But this is just *101*. There's still lots more to learn, both before you get married and for the rest of your life. That's where "listening to instruction" (see Proverbs 16:20) comes in. I have no doubt that as you start casting a vision of what you want your future family to look like, God is going to bring godly examples across your path, make His words jump off the page of your Bible, and help you find other books, blogs, and mentors who will contribute to your vision. You'll be learning how to do family well the rest of your life!

You'll never get to the end of learning new ways to do family well.

But regardless of the future, you've *already* come a long way. Think about it. I'd wager that you don't see family life the same way now as you did when you started page 1. God has done some cool stuff in your heart, and I want to give you a space to jot down some of the lessons, goals, and hopes you have for your future family.

In this next section, celebrate the changes God has made in your heart by dreaming about the future. I've put together a bunch of questions to help you cast a vision of what you'd like your family to look like someday, if your own family is what God has in store for you. This is your chance to really think through what you want most for your future family. So dream big and give it all prayerfully to God.

Family Dreams Quiz

1. Do you hope to have a family of your own someday?
    Why or why not? (All the questions from here on
    are based on an answer of yes to this one. But if you
    answered no, I think it would still be a good idea to
    answer these questions, just to get you thinking. You
    never know what God might do in the future!)

2. What habits, strengths, mind-sets, and victories have
    you seen in your current family that you also want to see
    in your future family?

3. How do you hope your future family will be different
    from your current family?

4. Write down five words that you hope will describe your home someday. (They could describe anything from the decor to your parenting style.)

5. What do you think it takes to have a good marriage?

6. What do you think will be the best part of finally being in charge as a parent?

7. How do you plan to you work out conflict with your husband?

8. How do you foresee disciplining and working out conflict with your kids?

9. If you were a fly on the wall watching your future family interact, what strengths would you hope to see in yourself?

10. What do you think will be the hardest part of being a wife?

11. What do you think will be the hardest part of being a parent?

12. What three things could you start working on now to prepare yourself for the challenges that will come in your future family?

13. Where are three wise places you could get help in shaping your ideas about a healthy, God-honoring family?

The Possible Impossible

If you're in the middle of, or have come from, a rough family situation, those dreams you just wrote down might feel next to impossible. Or maybe there's no "next to" about it—they just seem *totally* impossible. If so, maybe you can relate to Jairus.

Jairus was kind of a big shot in his town along the shore of Lake Galilee because he was a leader at the local synagogue, which means he was kind of like a pastor in a small town. People knew him, and people knew his family. (As most small-town pastors can sympathize with, people probably knew more about him than he wished they knew.)

Jairus had a twelve-year-old daughter, an only daughter,

and he loved her a lot. I don't know if they always got along, but I imagine that when she became sick, like *really* sick, whatever tension there had been between them evaporated like dew off a rooftop. Sickness has a way of putting relationships in the right perspective.

Jairus knew that if something didn't change, his little girl was going to die. He couldn't let that happen. He had already tried everything he could think of—everything except finding the Healer. Jairus knew that Jesus had a *supernatural* ability to heal sick people, so when he found out Jesus had just entered the town, he knew he had to do everything he could to get Him to come to his house. It seemed next to impossible, but someone with a desperate dream is willing to take big chances.

After quite a struggle, he finally made his way through a big group of people and threw himself at Jesus' feet. He cried. He pleaded. He begged Jesus to come to his house and heal his little girl.

Jesus said *yes*.

The next to impossible seemed to be happening.

But while they were on the way to his house, Jesus stopped for someone else. And while the Healer was giving fresh life to another suffering person, Jairus's own little girl died. Messengers came from his house and told him, "Your daughter is dead. There's no use troubling the Teacher now."

Next to impossible was replaced by just plain impossible.

Can you imagine how final that news must have felt? I mean, there's no changing death. There was absolutely nothing Jairus could do to bring his daughter back.

Can you relate? Does your family situation feel impossible to overcome? Does it seem like there's absolutely nothing you can do to change the way your family treats you or each other? Do you worry that you'll put your future kids through the same things you've suffered through? When you think about having a healthy family—now or in the future—does it seem *impossible*?

Lucky for Jairus—and lucky for you and me—Jesus is in the business of blowing just plain impossible right out of the water.

Jairus's daughter was dead. Really dead. Healing doesn't get more impossible than that. Yet Jesus looked at Jairus and said, "Don't be afraid. Just have faith, and she will be healed" (Luke 8:50).

In the face of ridiculously brutal odds, Jairus did have faith. He walked Jesus back to his house and showed Him to his dead daughter's room, because a desperate dream and living faith are *both* willing to take big chances.

When Jesus took that young girl's hand and presented her *alive* to Jairus, his joy must have been over the top! His faith, combined with God's ability, made the impossible possible.[9] Can you imagine how Jairus must have felt? I would have been jumping up and down and screaming/blubbering for all the town to hear.

Do you believe that God can do the same for you? Do you believe He can breathe new life into a "dead" family? Do you believe He can change your heart so that cycles of sin, pain, and dysfunction end with you?

"Don't be afraid. Just have faith."

There's a whole lot packed into those six words.

Go ahead and read them again: "Don't be afraid. Just have faith."

I recently had a conversation with a friend of mine about her story and how it relates to Jairus's. Her first family—the family she grew up with—fell apart at the seams. Betrayal, hurt, unfair expectations, depression, and death chopped up her family like a Benihana chef dices up dinner. From all practical standpoints, her new family—she, her husband, and two kids—should have been doomed to failure. The dysfunction she naturally learned from her parents should have carried over into her new family, making it a prime candidate for adultery, divorce, hate, and broken dreams. Thankfully, my friend took Jesus' words to heart. Instead of being afraid, she has been courageous. Instead of doubting what God can do, she has prayed for miracles. And her new family is a living example of grace, commitment, and love in action. If you met her, you'd never know the crazy past she had to overcome.

Stories like hers make me want to cheer! Stories like mine. Stories like the one you can write in your own life.

In that conversation with my friend, I asked her what advice she would give girls who have witnessed the worst sides of family. Here's what she said:

Everything we face can lead us closer to God if we'll let it, giving our pain purpose. You have to get to a place in life where you trust God completely with it all. When we stand in eternity someday and look back over our lives, we won't scrunch up our noses and say, "Well, that doesn't make any sense. Why would God do or allow that?" At that moment, we will see what it means that He works everything together for our good.

Her inspiring words bring us full circle, right back to the secret I shared with you at the beginning of our journey together. If you'll let Him, God will use *everything* in your life—including crummy family junk—for your good. Remember what the biggest "good" is? Becoming more like Jesus Christ.

- Loving like He loves you.
- Forgiving like He forgives you.
- Showing compassion like He offers you.
- Being humble, just as He is.
- Being patient, as He has been patient with you.
- Setting an example for others, just as He's shown you.

What better place to learn and practice all of that than in your messy, quirky, cracked-but-unique family?

So love well the people you call family, drawing from the love of Jesus inside you, and see if they don't start to like you back (wink).

Father, as I learn to give You more and more of my life, make me like Jesus. I want to be changed by Your love so that I can love my family well. Retrain my thinking so it's in line with Your best plan for my future family. I want to carry on a legacy of just how beautiful family

life can be. Show me how to start putting everything
I've learned into practice. I want to make You proud,
Daddy. Amen.

Application Questions

1. *What characteristics or experiences of your family are you*
   afraid you'll take with you to your future family?

2. *Do you think it's possible for someone to relearn how to do*
   family and break a cycle of brokenness? If so, what would it
   probably take to accomplish change?

3. *According to Proverbs 16:20, what is one key to breaking*
   unhealthy family legacies?

4. *What does Jairus's story teach us about God's ability to do the impossible?*

5. *I asked this question at the end of chapter 1, but now that you have ten more chapters under your belt, can you see any ways that God might be using the stuff you've faced (or are still facing) to make you more like Christ?*

6. *Take out your journal one last time. Write a prayer to God, asking Him for help with the things in your family you struggle with and giving Him your hopes and dreams for your future family.*

Question Time:
Getting to Know Your Parents

TO HELP YOU see your parents in a new light, I've put together some questions for you to ask your mom and dad that you might not otherwise ask. You can look at it as a little homework assignment. Pick a time and place when you can be alone to talk one-on-one.

I've put together eight questions to get you started; you get to come up with questions 9 and 10. Maybe there's a question you've always wanted to ask Mom or Dad that you've never had the opportunity (or courage) to ask. If you're not sure what to ask, questions 1 through 8 might help generate some new ideas.

A little side note before you begin: If you and your parents rarely communicate about more than daily business, this may be a little out of your comfort zone. You might feel awkward starting out, but don't let that stop you! As you go along, it will get easier for both of you, and by the end, you'll probably feel more comfortable than when you started.

Questions for Mom

1. What did you like to do after school when you were my age?

2. What's your happiest memory?

3. How was your relationship with your parents when you were a teen?

4. Who was your first romantic relationship with?

5. How did you become a Christian? (If you know that your mom isn't a Christian, you could ask a different question about spirituality, such as "What do you think happens to us when we die?")

6. What was your favorite subject in high school? Why?

7. How did you and Dad meet?

8. When you were growing up, what dreams and goals did you have for your life that you have since accomplished? What dreams and goals do you have yet to accomplish?

9.

10.

Questions for Dad

1. What was your first car like?

2. What's your happiest memory?

3. How was your relationship with your parents when you were a teen?

4. Tell me about your high school experience. Did you like it? What were you involved in?

5. How did you become a Christian? (If you know that your dad isn't a Christian, you could ask a different question about spirituality, such as "What do you think happens to us when we die?")

6. Who did you look up to most when you were growing up?

7. Were you nervous to ask Mom out on your first date? Where did you take her?

8. When you were growing up, what dreams and goals did you have for your life that you have since accomplished? What dreams and goals do you have yet to accomplish?

9.

10.

"Can I Be Trusted?" Quiz

1. Whether it was two years ago or last week, have you given your parents any reason to question whether they can trust you? How?

2. What sorts of choices do you think would make your parents more confident in trusting you? Name at least three wise choices you could make.

3. Was there a time (or season in your life) when you didn't use good judgment and got into some trouble?

4. Do you ask to do things that might make your parents feel as though you're not ready to have the freedom you crave (e.g., insisting on going to a party where no adults will be present)?

5. Are you secretive with e-mail, text messages, social media, friends, places you go, or details about your day?

6. Can you think of any ways you would personally benefit from being *less* private in order to secure your parents' trust?

7. Could you use some improvement in being thoughtful of your mom's and dad's feelings and rights as parents? How so?

8. Do you ever bend the truth to manipulate your parents into letting you do what you want? How?

9. When your parents tell you no, how do you usually respond? How could you respond that would let them see you're mature enough to handle more freedom?

The "Me" Quiz II

HIDDEN-GEM ALERT! LOVE quizzes? If you're a big sister, not a sister, or otherwise didn't read the chapter for little sisters, you missed a really fun one! Flip back to page 131 and take the quiz. It's not just for little sisters!

A Big Thank-You

In the fall of 2012, I sat at a table at Marigold Café in Colorado Springs, Colorado, with a team from NavPress to talk about an idea for a series of books for teen girls. It was raw, and I was nervous. Coincidentally, I choked on a peppercorn from my salmon-and-spinach salad and coughed so hard that a lady three tables away offered me an herbal drop from her purse. *Way to make a great first impression.* Luckily for me, my new friends saw past my inability to eat like a lady and caught the vision for the LIFE, LOVE & GOD series. Almost immediately, these four books ceased to be *my* project and became *ours. Crushed, Unashamed, Backwards Beauty,* and *Family* have been a team effort. And even though team members have subbed in and out, the fact remains that I could not have survived writing these four books without the amazing people God put in my corner. (My gratitude to *Him* is implied in every line.)

My husband, Paul, has been a stalwart support—not only encouraging me with his words, but playing Dad *and* Mom on one of his days off *for three years* so I could hole up at a rotating list of coffee shops to write nearly two hundred thousand words. For those of you who love LifeLoveandGod.com, he is also the resident tech/video/web/graphics guru in this operation. I *literally* couldn't do this without him!

My daughters, Ryan Kailey and Logan Cassidy, have had to share me with a whole bunch of girls they've never met, but they've handled it like the incredible little Christ followers they are. I'm amazed by their willingness to make sacrifices for the good of God's Kingdom. I love you, girls!

Don Pape, Caitlyn Carlson, and the rest of NavPress, as well as Jeff Rustemeyer, Robin Bermel, Nicole Grimes, Alyssa Anderson, and the Tyndale House Publishers dream team—I couldn't have asked for better partners for these books. Seriously. Thank you for not only believing in this series but also for sticking your necks out for me personally. These books are what they are because of you, and I am truly indebted.

I am also grateful to Nicci Jordan Hubert, editor extraordinaire, who has kept me from saying (too many) dumb things and has polished these books like a pro; Andrew Wolgemuth, who goes way beyond as both agent and friend; Chrissy Wolgemuth, who jumped in to watch my kids when deadlines loomed and I wasn't sure how I was going to get it all done; and the many other friends who reviewed, contributed to, and prayed over the manuscripts.

I have been blessed with an amazing tribe of sisters at LifeLoveandGod.com, especially my *Between the Lines* newsletter family and launch team members. Thank you to each one of you for reading what I write, sending your questions, and loving me despite my quirks, inconsistencies, and overuse of exclamation points!!! I am so very honored to get to walk this journey called life with you.

With love and gratitude,

jessie

Notes

1. *Merriam-Webster's Collegiate Dictionary*, 11th ed., s.v. "honor."
2. *Merriam-Webster's Collegiate Dictionary*, 11th ed., s.v. "obey."
3. James Strong, *Strong's Exhaustive Concordance of the Bible* (Peabody, MA: Hendrickson Publishing, 2009), s.v. "*kawlal*," Hebrew #7043.
4. *Merriam-Webster's Collegiate Dictionary*, 11th ed., s.v. "considerate."
5. *Merriam-Webster's Collegiate Dictionary*, 11th ed. s.v. "model."
6. James Strong, *Strong's Exhaustive Concordance of the Bible*, s.v. "*agape*," Greek #26.
7. For more information about love languages, see Gary Chapman, *The Five Love Languages: The Secret to Love That Lasts* (Chicago: Northfield Publishing, 2010).
8. *Merriam-Webster's Collegiate Dictionary*, 11th ed., s.v. "communication."
9. Jairus's story is found in Mark 5:21-43 and Luke 8:40-56.

A Note from the Author

FOR TEN YEARS, I've been writing and speaking, praying with and encouraging teen girls to live in the sweet spot of God's will for their lives. I love people of both genders and all ages—and I write and speak for them too—but I have a special place in my heart for young women. It's that heartache-y passion for my little sisters that led me to launch LifeLoveandGod.com, a website where I've been answering girls' most personal questions since 2005. And it's the same passion that has led me to write, speak, and mentor teen and young women for more than ten years.

I live by the adage "My life is an open book." Sometimes that means sharing stories with an audience that should really be reserved for reality TV shows. Sometimes that means crying real tears while I type wildly at a corner table at Starbucks. God never asked me to share a shiny, cellophane-wrapped version of my life with the world, so I offer the real me with all my messy details, hoping that both my failures and triumphs will encourage you on your own faith journey.

Freedom and *grace* are two of my favorite things in life. I hope you'll find lots of both any time you pick up one of my books. Those gems also come with me when I speak (along with their awkward cousin *humor*).

I consider it the highest honor to share life with you—whether through books or on stage. If I could gather you close for a big hug, I would (and I don't even care if you're not a hugger—deal with it). I can't wait for the day we'll get to meet in person!

If you'd like to invite me to your event,
please shoot me a line at
LifeLoveandGod.com/speaking.

YOU'VE GOT QUESTIONS.
JESSIE HAS ANSWERS.

Connect with Jessie at
LifeLoveandGod.com

**WHERE GIRLS ASK AND GET ANSWERS TO QUESTIONS
ABOUT BOYS, FAMILY, FRIENDS, AND GOD.**